"One of us had to [...]
and bolts of what happ[...]
group. Most writers make it seem as if working in a magickal group is like falling off a log, when in fact, it is an extremely complex issue, with many subtle and dangerous pitfalls. Lisa Mc Sherry talks about what all of that means from a witch's perspective—in careful detail and plain English. For anyone who is thinking of forming or joining a magickal group, *Magickal Connections* is definitely a 'must read.'"

CAL GARRISON, AUTHOR OF THE OLD GIRLS' BOOK OF SPELLS, THE OLD GIRLS' BOOK OF DREAMS, AND WITCH ON THE GO.

"Wow—what a fantastic book! All I could think as I read it was, "Where was this book when I was just starting out in founding a group over forty years ago, and many times since?" Had I this book in hand over all those years, I certainly wouldn't have made the many mistakes I inevitably did, and my lifelong efforts at community-building and group leadership would have been so much more effective and successful!

Everywhere I turn in the magickal community, I see groups forming and breaking apart—and not always, sad to say, amicably. Just as with so many marriages, which begin with such passionate love and too often end horribly in bitterness and betrayal, we have long needed a world-class "marriage counselor" for Pagan and magickal groups. And now, in Lisa Mc Sherry, at last we have one.

Lisa has a deep understanding of the principles of leadership and group dynamics, and articulates them here in the most comprehensible presentation I've ever encountered. Her exquisite little meditations and other exercises are so elegantly crafted as to take you all the way down through the subconscious and right to the heart of the matter for transformative insights. This brilliant work has long been sorely needed in the worldwide magickal community, and I for one am deeply grateful to Lisa Mc Sherry for finally providing it to us. Every Pagan and magickal group leader should have this book, and it should shortly become dog-eared from continual reference!"

OBERON ZELL-RAVENHEART, FOUNDER AND PRIMATE, CHURCH OF ALL WORLDS, FOUNDER AND HEADMASTER, GREY SCHOOL OF WIZARDRY, AUTHOR OF GRIMOIRE FOR THE APPRENTICE WIZARD

"I thought I would write this book some 15 years ago but soon realized I lacked the background and experience and my curled and yellowed notes lie forgotten. Lisa has written that book clearly, concisely and without the double-speak so common in sociology. Anyone joining, leading or hoping someday to form a magical/religious group should get a copy."

GREY CAT, AUTHOR OF DEEPENING WITCHCRAFT, ADVANCING SKILLS AND KNOWLEDGE, AND CO-AUTHOR OF AMERICAN INDIAN CEREMONIES: WALKING THE GOOD RED ROAD AS WELL AS CHAPTERS IN THE FIRST TWO VOLUMES OF WITCHCRAFT TODAY.

"Problems with group dynamics are undoubtedly the most common reasons why magical groups fail. Magical Connections explains the essential element of group dynamics and applies it to the success of pagan gatherings, be they covens, circles, online groups, or just meet-ups. I believe the impact of this book will be profound in the pagan community, and I know I will apply its techniques to the administration of my Iseum."

REV. DENISE "DION-ISIS" DUMARS, CO-FOUNDER, THE ISEUM OF ISIS PAEDUSIS, AUTHOR OF BE BLESSED

"Drawing from the the psychology of group dynamics, her observation of a broad spectrum of Pagan covens and other worship groups, as well as her own experience in both terraspace and cyberspace magical groups, Lisa Mc Sherry has carefully and thoroughly synthesized the best ideas into a guidebook that even the group leader of 30 years' experience will find useful. She has cooked up a sustaining meat-and-potatoes stew, spiced with self-evaluations, exercises and rituals."

M. MACHA NIGHTMARE, AUTHOR, RITUALIST, LECTURER, CHAIR, PUBLIC MINISTRY DEPARTMENT, CHERRY HILL SEMINARY
WWW.MACHANIGHTMARE.COM, WWW.CHERRYHILLSEMINARY.ORG

Lisa Mc Sherry

MAGICKAL
CONNECTIONS

Creating a Lasting and
Healthy Spiritual Group

New
Page
BOOKS

A division of the Career Press, Inc.
Franklin Lakes, NJ

MAGICKAL CONNECTIONS
EDITED BY JODI BRANDON
TYPESET BY KATE HENCHES
Cover design by Scott Fray
Interior images by ClickArt 360,000 Image Pak
Printed in the U.S.A. by Book-mart Press

To order this title, please call toll-free 1-800-CAREER-1 (NJ and
Canada: 201-848-0310) to order using VISA or MasterCard, or for further
information on books from Career Press.

The Career Press, Inc., 3 Tice Road, PO Box 687,
Franklin Lakes, NJ 07417
www.careerpress.com
www.newpagebooks.com

Library of Congress Cataloging-in-Publication Data
Mc Sherry, Lisa.
    Magickal connections : creating a lasting and healthy spiritual
group / by Lisa Mc Sherry.
        p. cm.
    Includes index.
    ISBN-13: 978-156414-932-9
    ISBN-10: 1-56414-932-3
        1. Occultism—Social aspects. 2. Social groups. I. Title.

BF1439.M37 2007
206--dc22

                                            2006038054

DEDICATION

We never do it alone. We live in a web of support from those near and far. This Dedication is first and foremost to everyone in my Community who chooses the hard path over the easy, the path of growth over remaining in place. I can only hope to be one of the many Guides you find along that Way. It is also for all the members of JaguarMoon Coven—past, present and future.
Without you, this book would not exist.

My parents, in their unique and separate ways, played a major role in this book. Their skills, opposite and complimentary, opened my beginners' mind. Most of all, this is for John—reader extraordinaire, my favorite, and a true partner.
"Moo" darling. Let's put this one into the foyer.

CONTENTS

INTRODUCTION

In 1999, I published an e-book, *CyberCoven.Org: Creating and Maintaining Magickal Groups Online*. Approximately half of that was later published as *The Virtual Pagan: Exploring Wicca And Paganism Through The Internet* (Red Wheel/ Weiser, 2002). At the same time the e-book came out, I began speaking at Pagan gatherings such as PantheaCon (held in February, in San Jose, California) on the topic of magickal group dynamics, a workshop I have given every year since then. Those workshops made me realize that the Pagan community needed a practical, accessible workbook, one that examines the group within the context of being a magickal group and how it can best be managed. *Magickal Connections* is the result.

I am a Pagan, a Priestess, and a Witch in varying combinations according to the circumstances. My perspective and background is rooted within the understanding of Deity, religion, community, symbols, and practices embodied within those terms. They are the context for my own mentoring and how I mentor others. It is not my intention to discuss Pagan traditions in any depth, and the reader must provide his or her own context for some of the practices I will discuss. To that end, I will occasionally make a sweeping statement about Paganism that will not be 100-percent true for every Pagan. I will do my best to avoid the situation, but I hope the reader will take it as a generalization rather that a statement of fact. As well, it may be that your temple/grove/coven/circle provides a structure for a process that is valuable and my perspective will be at odds with that. Don't toss your process! I have not written this book believing that everything I impart will be profoundly new. Instead, it is my intention to direct the reader's attention to generally accepted truths and cast them in a new light.

This book is about relationships. When I became the leader of my coven I was comfortable with my knowledge of magick, ritual, and teaching, but completely untutored in the dynamics and energy flows of a group. For various reasons, getting that training from my former High Priestess was not possible (including the fact that she held seriously to the old Law of silence once a coven has hived off from the mother coven), so I went looking into the literature. The topic of "group dynamics" has become very popular in the last decade, with a broad group of psychologists, sociologists, computer engineers, and systems analysts looking at the topic from the background of their own perspective and training and offering up texts and tomes of information. Into this mix a few books from the religious perspective have entered: Haugh's *Antagonists of the Church,* Farrell's *Gathering the Magic*, and Harrow's *Spiritual Mentoring* are a few examples.[1] Many other books within the Pagan community touch on aspects of group dynamics (GreyCat's chapter on building community comes to mind as

~Introduction~

an example[2]) but tend to leave the reader wanting more—the way a perfect appetizer does.

In the grand tradition of forerunners throughout time, I wanted something that didn't exist yet, and so I had to create it myself. Fortunately my background in psychology and sociology gave me a starting point for research, my ongoing involvement with the people of JaguarMoon, my coven, gave me a safe place to apply what I learned, and the people of the Pagan community with whom I shared my theories gave me validation. Those generous people—in Dianic circles, Discordian gabs, traditional covens, new-formed groves, current solitaries, temples, and free-floating groups—listened to my theories, provided feedback, and sent me off into new directions. What you hold in your hands now is a compilation of that research and testing from nearly a decade of work on my part. As produced here, the way seems clear and direct, but my journey was a confusing tangle of loops and side branches into areas that ultimately proved interesting, but beside the point.

> THROUGHOUT THE CHAPTERS YOU WILL FIND BOXES SIMILAR TO THIS ONE. THEY DENOTE EXERCISES RELATED TO THE CURRENT TOPIC. THESE EXERCISES MIGHT BE TO HELP YOU DELVE A LITTLE DEEPER INTO YOUR ATTITUDES AND BELIEFS, OR TO GIVE TO PEOPLE YOU ARE WORKING WITH START PERTINENT DISCUSSIONS. THEY ARE NOT REQUIRED, BUT ARE VALUABLE TOOLS FOR YOUR UNDERSTANDING AND DEVELOPMENT.

Each chapter of this workbook focuses on a different area of group dynamics: structures, functions, roles, mentoring, leadership, the group mind, life cycle of the group, and potential problems. Throughout, I have provided exercises to assist group members in defining and clarifying each area, as well as potential solutions. There are several rituals I have created and used in clarifying my own group's processes, and these are included as well.

~Magickal Connections~

Because much of my recent magickal group experience is in cyberspace, a hard-core learning experience for effective communication, there is specific information throughout it that is specific to virtual groups. In my experience, cyber groups are much harder to maintain and grow than physical groups, but the strategies are similar. If you are interested in taking your physical group online, see Appendix E for assistance.

I fully expect that this workbook will grow and expand over the years, and I encourage readers to contact me with their feedback, experiences, and solutions. I see this workbook as the beginning of an interactive relationship between the reader and myself—one that supports us both, helping us to achieve better results in all of the groups we participate in.

May the God/dess bless your Work!

Lisa Mc Sherry

Lammas 2006

CHAPTER 1

WHAT IS
A GROUP?

*Start by doing what's necessary; then do what's possible;
and suddenly you are doing the impossible.*
— *St. Francis of Assisi*

My fascination with groups and their participants began
in my undergrad days when I majored in psychology and mi-
nored in sociology. As a witch in a culture of partying and
middle-class norms, I found myself in the uncomfortable position of interacting with large, amorphous, mundane groups
that had rules and expectations I could understand, but never
belonged to. That feeling of disassociation persisted until I
found a traditionally based coven a decade ago.

When I began my own coven, I also began a process of
trial and error in learning how to participate in various situations. I learned what works, when, and what doesn't. As I
looked for sources of help in the larger magickal community
I began to realize that we lack consistent formal training in
group leadership. If we are lucky, we have an opportunity to
work with a longtime leader who is skilled in handling many

aspects of group dynamics. There aren't many of those leaders around. Most of us receive training the way I did: from a highly knowledgeable, magickally skilled person who lacked more than basic leadership abilities.

Group dynamics is the art of relationships, of making connections, a system that describes skills to use in various situations. We relate to one another because we must: We are fundamentally social creatures. Life demands it; life itself is a relationship. These situations range from your everyday encounters with near or total strangers to those where you are engaging in profound acts of intimacy. From the moment we enter the world we are forming relationships and being formed by them. My desire is to share with you what I have learned about working in and with a group. Otherwise, I fear that all of the pain, self-doubt, fear, failures, joy, and success I have experienced will only benefit myself.

For centuries, sages and scholars have been fascinated by groups: the way they form, change over time, dissipate unexpectedly, achieve great goals, and sometimes commit great wrongs. Humans are social animals: We naturally gravitate away from isolated circumstances into groups. But what, precisely, is a group? Is it all women in Seattle with blue eyes? An assistant talking with a manager by telephone? People waiting in silence at a bus stop? Spectators at a football game? Worshipers at a religious service?

Almost all of our time is spent interacting in groups; we are educated in groups, we work in groups, we worship in groups, and we play in groups. But even though we live our lives in groups, we often take them for granted. A group of people working in the same room, or on a common project, does not necessarily invoke the group dynamic. If the group is managed in a totally autocratic manner, there may be little opportunity for interaction relating to the work. If there are cliques and factions within the group, a cohesive process may never evolve. On the other hand, the group process may be utilized by distant individuals working on different areas; for instance, in a cyber magickal group.[1]

When people work in groups, there are two separate factors involved. The first is the *task* and the problems involved in getting the job done. For example: teaching a class, holding a ritual, or doing community outreach. Frequently, the task at hand is the only issue that the group considers. The second is the *process* of the group work itself: the mechanisms by which the group acts as a unit and not as a loose rabble. For example: How will we teach the class, what is involved, and who will do it? Without due attention to this process the value of the group can be diminished or even destroyed; yet with a little explicit management of the process, it can enhance the worth of the group to be many times the sum of the worth of its individuals. It is this *synergy* that makes group attractive despite the possible problems (and time spent).

In simple terms, a healthy, functioning magickal group leads to a spirit of cooperation, coordination, and commonly understood procedures and mores. If this is present within a group of people, their cohesion is enhanced by their mutual support (both practical and moral). Magickal groups can be particularly good at combining talents and providing innovative solutions to unfamiliar situations. The wider skill set and knowledge base found within a magickal group is a distinct advantage over that of a solitary practitioner. They are excellent environments for transmitting data across generations and keeping that information intact, while adding the wider experiences of its members.

Magickal groups are similar to relationships: You have to work at them. The responsibility for communication and development cannot rest on a single individual; it is an interactive flow between the leader(s) and participants. By making the group itself responsible for its own support, that responsibility becomes an accelerator for the overall group dynamic. What is vital is that these needs are recognized and explicitly dealt with by the group. Time and resources must be allocated by the entire group.

Groups and Their Influence

CONSIDER THE INFLUENCE PARTICIPATING IN VARIOUS GROUPS HAS ON YOU BY LISTING THE GROUPS TO WHICH YOU BELONG, AS WELL AS THOSE THAT INFLUENCE YOU.

1. MAKE A LIST OF ALL THE GROUPS YOU BELONG TO NOW. DON'T FORGET FAMILY, CLUBS, SPORT TEAMS, CLASSES, SOCIAL GROUPS, FRIENDS, WORK TEAMS, AND SOCIAL CATEGORIES THAT ARE MEANINGFUL TO YOU (AMERICAN, WOMAN, WITCH, FALCONS FAN, AND SO ON).

2. DO ANY OF THE GROUPS YOU BELONG TO TRANSFORM MEMBERS INTO A UNIT THAT IS GREATER THAN THE SUM OF ITS PARTS?

3. WHICH GROUP HAS CHANGED THE MOST OVER TIME? DESCRIBE THIS CHANGE BRIEFLY.

4. WHICH GROUP HAS INFLUENCED YOU, AS AN INDIVIDUAL, THE MOST? HOW SO?

5. IDENTIFY FIVE GROUPS THAT YOU DO NOT BELONG TO, BUT THAT INFLUENCE YOU IN SOME WAY (FOR EXAMPLE, REPUBLICAN). OF THESE GROUPS, WHICH ONES INFLUENCE YOU—YOUR BEHAVIORS, EMOTIONS, OR DECISIONS—THE MOST?

An adequate definition of "group" must strike a balance between being sufficiently broad to include most social collectives that are true groups and being sufficiently narrow to exclude the collectives that are not true groups. A formal definition meets this criteria: "A group is (a) two or more individuals

(b) who influence each other (c) through social interaction."[2] Some theorists add a fourth element, that of having common goals, but that makes the definition too narrow. Can something so scientific be applied to magickal groups, those fluid, changing, fantastical creations that seem to exist without rules, or even despite them? Yes. (It is worth pointing out here that being a group is not necessarily something to strive for; it's a useful definition and label.)

We humans are social creatures, and it is inevitable that when we come together in groups we will encounter conflict. For most of us, the word *conflict* conjures images of shouting, tense muscles, and often fear. But conflict can be valuable, and there are many group situations that benefit from disagreements, if handled well. Together we will look at forms of conflict, root causes, and skills to manage the tensions to produce a positive outcome.

Magickal Group Structures

Things which matter most should never be at the mercy of things which matter least.

—*Johann von Goethe*

I practiced as a solitary for years. In the beginning, it was because I lived at home and had no freedom to find like-minded Pagans. Through the years, I found myself going to public circles with increasing frequency until I eventually joined a large "open" circle in Sacramento. The lack of organization frustrated me, and when a five-week Shamanic workshop I was in looked to recombine as a closed circle I jumped at the opportunity. We began as a hierarchical group, but transmuted into a circle of equals and worked together, deepening our skills for several years. I found working with others to be an exhilarating and occasionally exasperating experience. For example, when we spent a month working with Faeries, I was bored (sorry, but I was) because it felt too fluffy.[3] Yet when Otterwoman led us in a concentrated exploration of our power animals during her month I learned many new things and wanted it to continue for months longer. Eventually I moved from the area and returned to my solitary practice once again.

In the mid-90s I joined ShadowMoon coven and began to study Wicca on a formal basis. My teacher, Lady Mystara, made no bones about the fact that she thought I would make an excellent High Priestess one day, and that day would come sooner than I thought. Frankly, I thought she was being sweet and supportive, but wrong. As a solitaire, the idea of becoming the leader of a group never occurred to me. Although in my time with the group I took my turn at leading rituals and designing lessons, the role of leader never seemed to "fit" me very well. But the Initiations I underwent opened up aspects of my Self that I previously thought were pipe dreams and a child's fantasies. I moved deeper into my core being, and found new Paths opening up for me the deeper in that I journeyed. And when I first conceived the fact of my magickal group, I believed that I would be leading it alone, forming it with members entirely unknown to me (because that was the Tradition). As a result, much of my early planning was based on the idea that I had to "go it alone."

But the God/dess willed differently.[4] Two former coven siblings and my best friend all contacted me within a few months to tell me they wished to be a part of creating a new magickal group. We talked online, and over the phone, in conference, and singly. These conversations turned into concrete goals and commitments as we each identified roles we would take and skills we would use to support the magickal group in the best way possible. I may have been the birthing mother, but the four of us were the parents of the new entity. It may have been un-Traditional, but this process is now a part of my own Tradition.

~What Is a Group?~

Within the Craft there are a range of group structures, from freeform to strictly hierarchical, with several variations in between. Each type of structure has its own requirements, and choosing which style best suits your personality and vision is crucial to creating or participating in a successful magickal group. The key question to ask is: How much structure do I/we need? Think about where your strengths draw you. You may prefer the clear authority of the hierarchy, the intuitive, flowing feeling of a freeform group, or perhaps something in between.

For the sake of discussion, I have divided the myriad types of magickal groups into four basic structures: hierarchical, circle, wheel, and freeform. These labels are not intended to be anything other than guideposts, terms that allow me to discuss the pros and cons of these different styles. Throughout my years as a witch I have personally witnessed the positive and negative aspects of each kind of group.

Hierarchical

A hierarchical group is one in which structure and codified knowledge plays an important role, even if it seems to be "made up" as the magickal group members go along. Generally speaking, no matter how small the group is, there is one person in the role of High Priestess, a single leader responsible for most, if not all, decision-making within the group. There may or may not be a co-leader (either the High Priest or Maiden). In a large group, these roles could be expanded to include Elders, a Scribe, a Knight (the male equivalent of a Maiden), a Treasurer, and other such titles of authority (see Creating a Supportive Magickal Group, page 30). These roles are assigned to individuals and, in most cases, are not rotated through the membership. Most certainly, the role of the High Priestess does not shift to different individuals, except on rare occasions when the Maiden or High Priest performs a ritual. The image associated with this structure is that of a triangle.

~Magickal Connections~

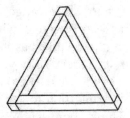

HIERARCHICAL MAGICKAL GROUP

Hierarchical magickal groups generally have specific definitions for each member's level of learning. Most often these are expressed as:

- ◉ Seeker—completely new to the Craft.
- ◉ Dedicant—has some Craft learning, but wishes to study specifically within the magickal group's tradition.
- ◉ Degree(d)—initiated, and at some level of priesthood.

Hierarchical magickal groups tend not to advertise actively for new members and are fairly specific about what kind of person they feel is most appropriate as a candidate to join. They frequently ask for a commitment of a year and a day as a Seeker or Dedicant before considering the candidate to be a member of the magickal group. Hierarchical groups will either view advancement through the Degrees or continual (measurable) improvement of the Self as the primary reason for participation in the magickal group. Degrees are only granted after specific types of knowledge and magickal mastery are demonstrated.

The model for this type of group most closely resembles a traditional (Abrahamic) Church although the belief that a Priest/ess's authority is derived from being "closer" to the God/dess than other members is not the same. Decisions flow from the top downward, with communication (and, particularly, change) flowing more easily through the lower levels than upward. It takes a particularly even-handed and open-minded leader to function well in this structure. The triangle easily leads to an extremely authoritarian model in which the leader has power over the other members, rather than sharing power with them.[5] The triangle, however, provides clear lines of authority and decision-making. The triangle is a very stable structure, as the late Buckminster Fuller noted. (He applied pressure to both a rectangle and a triangle. The rectangle folded up and became unstable, but the triangle withstood the pressure and was twice as strong.) Hierarchy is a common form of dynamic in today's society, one that often feels comfortable. We know it well.

Deity is often conceptualized as a parental figure, particularly in the early stages of our coming to Paganism. It is a by-product of our understanding of deity as something not to be questioned, an authority to please. As we grow, we develop more meaningful relationships with our Deities in an ongoing process that reflects our own growth.

From this perspective, it is not too hard to see why a newcomer might prefer a hierarchical group to work with. The structure is easily seen, the lines of communication seemingly clear, and the process of evolution through the degrees, obvious. This is not to say that a hierarchical structure is less "evolved" than another organization. However, it feels safe and comfortable. Hierarchy is a structure most of us live within in most aspects of our lives; looking for it in our spiritual life is reflecting the structure we know. Training in such a magickal group provides a solid background in ritual writing, participation, and leading, as well as a thorough grounding in the Mysteries. After such training, members feel confident in their knowledge and are able to pass that knowledge on to others.

As I said earlier, all structures have potential problems. A hierarchical concept of Deity and priesthood can leave too much room for authorities to interpret what Deity wants. Usually this is unquestioning obedience, but sometimes it is the donation of resources (time or money) to the authorities' control. When hierarchy is an inherent part of religious belief, there is a system in place that allows the priesthood to claim to speak for Deity, and in doing so claim special privileges for itself. The triangle's downside is that negative politics and dynamics may prevent members from growing in self-knowledge and/or advancing through the Degrees. Some may be "promoted" although they have less knowledge, because they are "popular," or because they please the leader(s) in some fashion. Speaking against authority figures may be discouraged, although lip-service paid to all being equal. Members in positions of authority may enjoy the power gained too much and misuse it for personal pleasure, rather than for the good of the group. Hierarchies can breed stagnation, with new ideas and beliefs seen as "wrong" or "bad," and not accepted. The triangle is where one finds members saying that theirs is the One True Way, even if it is only by implication rather than an outright statement.

That said, my own magickal group began as a hierarchy, and often reverts to one during times of clearing/fire (see Chapter 7). When a group is just getting started, the triangle can be the most efficient, convenient, and powerful one to work within. The force of will of a single person is sufficient to found a new magickal group; when a group is small (or just starting), lines of communication are easy to create and maintain without the dynamic feeling such as one of hierarchy.

Circles

"Circle" is a very broad concept, one that is inclusive of the huge continuum of magickal groups between hierarchical and freeform. A circle can best described as a gathering of people for a specific purpose—worship of the Deity, learning the Craft, casting spells, developing psychic abilities, and so forth. Although they may have roles like a hierarchical magickal group, circles will also tend to have rotating leaders, with several, or all, of the members of the group taking turns in that position.

CIRCULAR MAGICKAL GROUP

Most circles do not have a formal system of progression from beginner to advanced practitioner. But, if they do, they will generally confer few titles upon their members. They may or may not follow a Tradition, and are more likely to be eclectic, borrowing and re-creating rituals and practices from many sources. The training received in this situation will be very practical—a matter of "do what works," rather than "our teachings say" will most likely be the guiding philosophy.

Some roles may be assigned on a rotating basis, with responsibility for details and organization spread among many members. This is an excellent situation in which to explore a variety of roles with many permutations. Each member contributes differently. Multiple sources of information are accessed, depending on the leaders' background, philosophy, and prior training. As well, a variety of perspectives can be presented as equally valid. The membership is generally rather stable, and there probably will be an agreed-upon process of taking in new members that involves some degree of screening.

~Magickal Connections~

Circles are valuable structures when the group wishes to explore non-hierarchical and empowering methods of dynamics. Many feminist Witches, such as Starhawk and Diane Stein, believe that the best way to break out of the "programming" of daily life is to enact circles magickally, constantly. And they make a very good point. We live in a world of triangles—hierarchies—all around us. At work, at home, in nearly every aspect of our lives we exist within a triangle of power-over. For some people, the shared responsibility and leadership of a circle is a vital component to healing and empowerment.

The negative side to this style is that if the circle does not have a strong core of members, it may lack sufficient organization. Lessons may be excellent or mediocre, depending entirely upon the personal knowledge of the teacher. Members may never see the "big picture" or grasp that there is more knowledge to be learned than that taught by the circle. A lack of a single leader may lead to petty squabbles and no person feeling empowered to say "enough!" The rotating leadership may contribute to a feeling of chaos if each imposes his or her personal vision upon the circle. An agreed-upon vision would help prevent this latter situation. Circles may also do a disservice to those people who are "natural" leaders or organizers. They may end up feeling stymied or held back by the circles' inherent lack of formal structure.

Wheel

Borrowing some of the best from hierarchies and circles stands the wheel. It is also the most difficult structure to create, as we have very few models to refer to. The most well-known is that of Reclaiming Collective:

> THE RECLAIMING TRADITION IS A FORM OF MODERN, FEMINIST WITCHCRAFT WHICH WAS INITIALLY DEVELOPED IN THE CLASSES, WORK-SHOPS, SUMMER PROGRAMS AND PUBLIC RITUALS OF THE RECLAIMING COLLECTIVE (1978-1997). A LIVING RELIGION WHICH CONTINUES TO

~What Is a Group?~

EVOLVE, IT IS A BELIEF SYSTEM AND A STYLE OF RITUAL AND MAGIC, NOT A CHURCH OR ORGANIZATION WITH ANY KIND OF FORMAL MEMBERSHIP THAT ONE CAN "JOIN."...THE COLLECTIVE INVITED INPUT FROM THE ENTIRE COMMUNITY, WIDESPREAD DISCUSSIONS ENSUED, AND ANOTHER RETREAT WAS HELD IN NOVEMBER 1997...AT THE 1997 RETREAT THE RECLAIMING COLLECTIVE DISSOLVED ITSELF, CREATING BASIC SUGGESTIONS AND GUIDELINES FOR THE STRUCTURE OF RECLAIMING IN THE BAY AREA WHICH EXISTS TODAY, CONSISTING OF THE WHEEL, VARIOUS WORKING CELLS, AND THE ADVISORY COUNCIL. RECLAIMING WITCHES IN OTHER PLACES ORGANIZE THEMSELVES (OR NOT) AS THEY WILL. THERE IS NO CENTRAL AUTHORITY AND ALL WITCH CAMPS ARE AUTONOMOUS.

THE WHEEL OF RECLAIMING TODAY HOLDS THE LEGAL IDENTITY OF RECLAIMING AS A TAX-EXEMPT RELIGIOUS ORGANIZATION. ITS MEMBERS ARE CHOSEN BY THE WORKING GROUPS, KNOWN AS "CELLS," WHO DO VARIOUS PROJECTS IN THE NAME OF RECLAIMING. FOR EXAMPLE, THE CELL THAT PUBLISHES THE RECLAIMING QUARTERLY, THE CELL THAT TEACHES CORE CLASSES, AND THE CELL THAT WORKS ON SPECIAL, ONE-TIME PROJECTS EACH HAVE A REPRESENTATIVE ON THE WHEEL. THE WHEEL MAKES DECISIONS BY CONSENSUS AND IS EMPOWERED TO ACT IN THE NAME OF RECLAIMING IN A LEGAL CONTEXT, TO MAKE POLICY DECISIONS, AND TO RECOGNIZE NEW CELLS.[6]

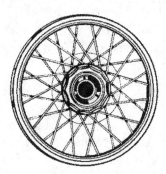

WHEEL MAGICKAL GROUP

The wheel derives its strength from having a stable "hub" of leadership, with equal divisions of responsibility radiating outward from the hub, and then spread among the larger membership.

~Magickal Connections~

As in a circle, roles may rotate among members. Each member contributes differently, and multiple sources of information are accessed, depending on the participants' backgrounds, philosophies, and prior training. As well, a variety of perspectives can be presented as equally valid.

The membership within a wheel is generally stable, and there is usually a process of taking in new members that involves some degree of screening and common agreement. Wheels tend to view advancement through the Degrees via the development of the Self as the primary reason for participation in the magickal group. Degrees are granted after specific types of knowledge and magickal mastery are demonstrated. Training provides a solid background in many areas of magickal knowledge, as well as a thorough grounding in the Mysteries. After such training, members feel confident in their knowledge and are able to pass that knowledge on to others.

The downside is that the membership can become too rigid in its views of what is "right" or acceptable to train and learn. A great deal of work may be done by few members, perhaps only those at the hub, with the reality being that this is a hierarchy, not a wheel. It also may be difficult for radical change to occur, with the illusion of transformation offered to those who desire it but then run afoul of a diffuse leadership unable to actually enact change.

Freeform

At the opposite end of the spectrum from hierarchy is the freeform structure. These groups are very informal, with membership generally in a state of flux; people show up or not as their lives allow. There is rarely any specific outlining of duties or roles, although a successful freeform group will probably have members who make sure the details are handled and that things are somewhat organized. Freeform groups have few if any rules and generally do not last very long. Frequently,

~What Is a Group?~

a freeform group will transmute into the more structured and stable circle and therefore last longer.

FREEFORM MAGICKAL GROUP

If you are interested in finding a situation in which to interact with a highly eclectic group of people, this style is perfect for you. Membership is fluid, with huge amounts of information shared over a wide range of topics. (Most e-mail lists that call themselves cyber magickal groups are actually freeform structures, in my opinion.)

The potential negatives for the freeform group are related to its lack of leadership. Where in a circle the leadership may feel chaotic or weak, it is nonetheless present and can be invoked. In a freeform group there is the potential for a covert leader to come into existence, with an attendant need for secrecy and behind-the-scenes manipulation. As well, there can be a total lack of guidance, direction, and support. A group that comes together with the best of intentions can drift into nothingness if it lacks all structure. Even Discordian and Anarchist groups have structure to allow them to get things done; if they do not, then by my earlier definition they are most likely not a group.

[It is interesting to note that the Reclaiming Collective is one of the few (perhaps the only) magickal group to have transformed itself from freeform—the original collective in 1982 where "the Collective consisted of anyone who knew someone to tell them when the next meeting was, and was willing to sit through that meeting" through the circle (arbitrarily when they attained 501(c)(3) status in 1994), into that of a wheel (by formal consensus decision in late 1997].[7]

Recognizing Structures

LIST THE STRUCTURES OF ORGANIZATIONS AND GROUPS, FORMAL AND INFORMAL WITHIN YOUR LIFE [YOU MAY WANT TO USE THE RESULTS FROM THE GROUPS AND THEIR INFLUENCE EXERCISE ON PAGE 16]. THIS CAN INCLUDE EMPLOYMENT, SCHOOLING, VOLUNTEER, AND SOCIAL ACTIVITIES. NEXT TO EACH ONE ANSWER WHETHER IT HAS A SINGLE LEADER, HOW INFORMATION FLOWS, AND WHERE YOU PLACE EACH MEMBER WITHIN THE STRUCTURE. WHERE DOES EACH FALL: HIERARCHICAL, CIRCLE, WHEEL, OR FREEFORM? DOES ANY SHIFT STRUCTURE? ARE THOSE SHIFTS PREDEFINED OR A RESPONSE TO GROUP NEEDS? HOW DO YOU FEEL ABOUT YOUR PLACE WITHIN THOSE STRUCTURES? WHAT DO YOU LIKE AND DISLIKE ABOUT EACH?

Group Functions

Theoretically, each type of magickal group structure can function perfectly, and many groups overlap, frequently beginning with one objective (for example, celebrate the eight Sabbats) and then acquiring new ones over time (such as, celebrate and provide public outreach services). In my magickal journeys, I have encountered four distinct kinds of groups:

1. **Ritual only.** Some magickal groups operate only to do ritual—either solar or lunar, making magic or simple worship. In my experience this kind of magickal group is very difficult to maintain online, rarely maintaining coherence for more than a year. Physical groups of this sort abound.

2. **Information Sharing.** Many magickal groups provide basic education in some (or many) aspects of

~What Is a Group?~

the faith and beliefs found under the Pagan "umbrella." Some also provide a place for like-minded Pagans to talk and share among peers. Members may not share the same views, but will be close enough in core principles to get along. Participants may take turns as teachers, and sharers of information.

3. **Teaching.** These magickal groups choose to focus either on a series of lessons, or on a specialization in one type of information (for example, herbalism) They tend to have either a set timeframe in which they present lessons, or a rotating collection that students may take as time allows. (Online, teaching groups may post lessons for anyone to do as they choose.) Many magickal groups fall into this category in that they desire to "pass the Tradition along" to members.

4. **Teen.** This type of magickal group is not necessarily structured differently from the other three, but is a phenomenon that deserves separate mention. Within these groups under-legal-age Witches meet others in the same age range, share information, and support one another. They can be very short-lived, but are immensely popular, especially online.

Group Experiences

SPEND TIME WRITING ABOUT YOUR THREE MOST COMMON GROUP EXPERIENCES. WHAT ARE THEY, HOW ARE THEY STRUCTURED, AND WHAT DO YOU LIKE AND DISLIKE ABOUT THOSE EXPERIENCES? WHAT GROUP EXPERIENCES DO YOU LIKE THE MOST? IS THAT GROUP ONE OF YOUR THREE MOST COMMON? IF NOT, WHY?

WHAT WAS THE LEAST POSITIVE GROUP EXPERIENCE YOU HAVE EVER HAD? WHAT WAS THAT GROUP'S STRUCTURE? ARE ANY OF THE GROUPS YOU ARE CURRENTLY IN SIMILAR TO THAT NEGATIVE EXPERIENCE?

~Magickal Connections~

Creating a Supportive Magickal Group

The more people you have to share the work, the larger and more stable your magickal group can be. Although a magickal group is not always democratic in its decision-making, and in the end a single person could lead the group alone, there are some roles that will make the group's existence healthier (and the leader's life easier!) if they are shared out among several people. From the outset, think of what part each member can play; setting the precedent of shared responsibility will never be as easy as at the beginning.

Although there are other titles and roles, I believe that the following is a good starting point. There is no reason to feel confined only to these positions. I suggest you choose roles that play to members' strengths as well as the group's needs.

Traditional Roles

Although individual groups may create roles particular to their needs and tradition, some titles are more common than others. The first two roles call for someone who has excellent organizational skills and are ideal for an individual who likes to track things. If, however, you are good at organizing and have the time to devote to it, then you may wish to do these tasks yourself. Remember, though, that the High Priest/ess wears many hats and must always be careful not to burn out.

An important role is that of a **Scribe**, a person who keeps track of group information such as ritual dates and times, lessons taught, files sent out, and so on. Ideally, this person would be able to re-send information that a member missed the first time around, or lost. Traditionally, this person also adds to the group's Book of Shadows, updating information, tracking ritual results, and expanding the repertoire of information available to members. (In a cyber group the Scribe may act in tandem with the Web Weaver. See the next section.)

Another important role is that of the **Handmaiden** or **Knight** (as appropriate to gender), who acts as the backup to the High Priest/ess in many areas of group administration and ritual. In a world where so much can change at the last minute, it is vital to have a person available who can step forward in the leaders' absence. The Handmaiden/Knight can act as counselors to the High Priest/ess, people you can always count on to give you their honest appraisal and good advice.

A **Calendar Keeper** tracks and maintains the groups' calendar (perhaps using an online calendar, or a shared e-mail program). The calendar may show ritual dates, class meetings, birthdays, or other events.

A **Coordinator** is responsible for creating meeting agendas, and taking notes of meetings and sharing them. The Coordinator may also maintain the group membership information (phone numbers, addresses, birthdays, and so on). In a small group the Scribe may take care of these duties.

A **Mentor** acts as a student's primary contact; monitors a student's responses and guides in appropriate direction (if needed); evaluates a student's progression through the lesson plan; and meets with students three times a year for one-on-one evaluations. If student joins the group, the mentor may act as the Sponsor. (More on this role in Chapter 6.)

A **Ritual Leader** (amazingly enough) leads rituals, primarily non-Sabbat, throughout the year; s/he may also write rituals. At the core, s/he understands the elemental forces summoned and manipulated, and can handle odd disruptions within the circle.

~Magickal Connections~

Modern Roles

If your group uses the Internet or Web to communicate or coordinate activities, you may want to look for members with a particular set of skills: technical. For example, in JaguarMoon at least one member holds the title of **Techno-Specialist.** Techno-Specialists are responsible for answering questions group members have about computer-related issues. An advanced knowledge of computers is not necessary, but they have to be comfortable using and working with various levels of technology, as well as having a solid understanding of computers and their operating systems. Ideally, they also know where to look for answers to questions they cannot answer.

The **Web Weaver** is responsible for all aspects of the group's Website, including any redesigns and updates, smooth navigation, easy viewing, and consistency of look and feel throughout the site. S/he handles issues with the Website on an ongoing basis.

Calling Your Group

If you are not currently working with a group, but want to (either as a member or leader), you can send out a *Call* to draw the right people to you, or manifest the perfect group.

Decide whether you are ready for leadership, or want to find the best group for you to work with. Do not specify a group that already exists, but describe the group you want in whatever detail feels right to you. (Marion Weinstein recommends adding the phrase "its equivalent or better" to Workings, and I think that is a wise idea in most cases.)

Cast a circle and create sacred space. Invoke your Deities and invite them to guide you to the perfect group (or assist in having others contact you). Get comfortable and

~What Is a Group?~

clear your mind of all distractions, including your intent. When you are clear, chant out loud, three times (first to announce your intention, second to state the goal, and the third to seal the desire):

If there be a perfect match,
this work tonight will surely catch.
The perfect ones, meant to be,
shall find their way to me.
In perfect love and perfect trust,
I send this out, and, as it must
this spell will guide us to unite,
So mote it be tonight!

Thank the Deities and other beings present; open the circle. Know that it is and that time will manifest the truth of that.

MAKING CONTACT

A quick survey of occult literature[1] indicates that magickal groups in modern times form in one of two ways: They are formed either by like-minded people who usually know one another personally, or by placing advertisements in Pagan-friendly journals. Membership is, for the most part, limited to physical geography. (Geography is not a limiting factor in a cyber group, and the process of advertising can be as simple as sending an e-mail.) Knowing what you want in a member will help define the screening process. The more clearly you know what your "ideal" is, the more likely you will see that person when he or she applies. Although joining a coven is not quite the same as applying for a job, there are some interesting similarities in the process to which both sides should pay attention in the interviewing process. The rest of this chapter is based on the assumption that you are starting a new group. The first thing to do is answer a set of questions:

~Magickal Connections~

- How do I to find members?
- What can I do to make sure they are compatible?
- Who will help with this endeavor?

Advertising

It's hard to start a group if you don't tell anyone about it. Sharing the news can be local, or region-wide; it can be via word of mouth or anonymous advertising. Even if you have no intention of using it, I recommend you create an advertisement.

Creating an Advertisement

TAKE OUT A LARGE PIECE OF PAPER (OR OPEN A TEXT EDITOR). TAKING A FEW MINUTES WITH EACH, ANSWER THESE QUESTIONS:

WHAT IS THE FIRST GOAL THAT NEEDS TO BE ACHIEVED? WHAT IS THE LONGEST-TERM GOAL? WHAT STYLE WILL YOU WORK IN?

REMEMBER: IF YOU ARE ONLY INTERESTED IN CREATING A CELTIC TRADITIONAL COVEN, THEN YOU ARE NOT TRYING TO ATTRACT PEOPLE PRIMARILY CONCERNED WITH NATIVE AMERICAN SHAMANISM. IS YOUR AD FOCUSED ENOUGH?

ARE YOU LOOKING FOR EXPERIENCED WITCHES TO SHARE KNOWLEDGE AND SUPPORT ONE ANOTHER AS THEY GROW IN THEIR KNOWLEDGE OF THE MYSTERIES? A GROUP OF NEOPHYTES? A MIXTURE OF BOTH?

Knowing what kind of people you want to attract will help you decide where you wish to post your invitation. Each magazine, Website, and list online has a different audience and there is no point advertising for your New Aeon Temple on the Traditional Witch list, for example—you will just irritate those members and waste your time. Before posting the ad, think about its wording and its elements. Is the tone excited, solemn, or anxious? Keep in mind that your invitation will be the first glimpse others will have of you, and first impressions are vital.

Here is an example of a physical advertisement to start a coven:

> "Experienced witch looking for new students with whom to share her knowledge. A one-year course of study will provide you with a knowledge of meditation, visualization, correspondences, ritual creation and performance, basic healing skills, the history of Wicca, and much more. You must be willing to commit to this learning on a daily basis as well as in weekly meetings. Please contact Maat at P.O. Box 123, Occult City, CA, 94666."

Notice how readers are told what they will learn, how long it will take, and the commitment required. The advertisement is a bit long, which costs more to place in a print medium, but you will probably have higher quality, more appropriate responses. There are several negatives, however. One is that it can take a while for your advertisement to be printed, as many journals only publish quarterly. By the time people have responded to your advertisement, met with you, and agreed to become members, a year may pass before the group can start. Another consideration is that the use of the word *Witch*, *Wicca*, or *witchcraft* may invite religious bigots to contact you and tell you that you are going to hell. If there is a high level of religious bigotry in your area, you may want to open a P.O. box.

Here is a list of places you could advertise for new members in the physical world:

- *Magickal Blend.*
- *SageWoman.*
- *PanGaia.*
- *The Beltane Papers.*

~Magickal Connections~

- *Pentacle Magazine*. (UK)
- *White Dragon*. (UK)
- *IF...Journal*.

A good magazine stand will provide you with further ideas. Local New Age journals, health magazines, feminist, or New Age bookstores, and cafés are also great sources and resources. Tell all your friends, and have them tell all of their friends as well! If there is a university or college nearby, place notices on its bulletin boards and consider advertising in the campus newspaper. (Note, however, that many campuses regulate use of their bulletin boards. With the rise of hate crimes, many now require posters be approved first.)

An electronic ad is very different because it's not limited to the amount of space you can buy, or a publication's schedule. An electronic ad might read as follows:

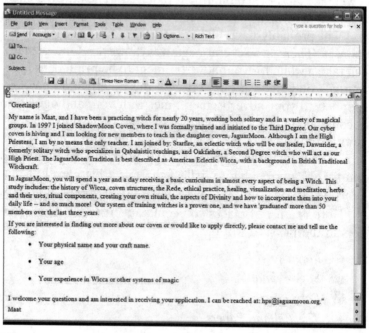

~Making Contact~

Clearly, doing an online advertisement is much more fun! You can tell your audience much more about yourself and what you are doing. But it costs you no more than the electrons transmitted via modem—nearly nothing if you are already online. You will also reach a much larger group of people faster. In the first year, ShadowMoon had nearly 100 applications for the class, of which 38 people were chosen. In our second year we had nearly 200 applications and increased our size to 50. JaguarMoon always receives more than 50 applications for the class and it is always difficult for us to choose which students we can accept. (It varies by the number of active members.)

A note about style: When writing your advertisement, whether for print or online, make sure at least one other person reads the copy before you submit it. Have him or her look for spelling, punctuation, and grammatical errors. Ask her/him to tell you how s/he feels about you after reading the ad: Are you portraying yourself as someone you're not? It's easy to come across as pompous in print! Online resources for placing advertisements are:

- ◎ *WitchVox* (*www.witchvox.com*): This is a Website with a variety of places for "announcing" your coven.

- ◎ *Yahoo!Groups* (*www.yahoogroups.com*): This a list service, hosting a huge number of Pagan-friendly lists. Some of these lists are open to posts from non-members; others are more private.

If you send your advertisement to a list service, always speak with the moderator or manager and make sure that you are welcome. Some lists consider advertising rude.

~Magickal Connections~

Teaching: An Alternative

You may want to consider holding a series of "101" classes as a way to get to know people and to work with them prior to formally starting a magickal group. Announce that you will be teaching these classes in a variety of places, perhaps both physical and online, and see who shows up. You may find the nucleus of your new group in these classes, particularly if you wish to form a teaching or information sharing coven. If the lesson is to take place in a physical location, see if you can hold it in a neutral location—a New Age spirituality store, a candle shop, or even in a room at your local library. I strongly recommend not holding it in your home; you do not know who will attend—and who will then be able to return later.

Welcoming Mercury and Hesta in to Your Life

Here is a ritual designed to increase your success at forming a coven, at drawing interesting and stable members, and at speeding the process.

Cleanse your self and your sacred space. Call the quarters, focusing on: Air's quality of inspiration and new beginnings, Fire's energy, Water's intuitive link to the psychic realm, and Earth's ability to reveal secrets.

Invoke Mercury and Hesta:

"Lady of the Hearth, Goddess of the Meeting Place
Hesta!
Quiet Goddess of Hospitality I call to You
Join my Circle tonight!
Lord of Air, Master of Communication
Mercury!

~Making Contact~

Silver-tongued God I call to You
Join my circle tonight!
Lord and Lady I ask that you stand
Hosts to my coven-to-be
Join with me to welcome those who will
Join my new family!
As I will, So Mote it Be!"

Get comfortable, either sitting upright, perhaps in a chair, or lying comfortably upon the floor.

Breathe deep for a long count and let any tension within your body release. Relax and grow still. Breathe deeply again and feel yourself slipping into a trance.

You are standing on a path in a field. It is evening, and you are headed home. Steadily you walk the path: It is familiar to you and your feet know the way. As you come over a low hill, you come suddenly upon a house. The path leads to its door. You walk to the door and raise your hand to knock.

Before you can do so, the door opens and a young man looks out at you. He is grinning, and you feel yourself smile in response. "I thought I heard your step," he says to you. "Welcome...well-come indeed," so saying he opens the door wider and gestures you inside.

The floor is polished wood, smooth underfoot. A fire is laid within the hearth and the smell of something delicious cooking makes your mouth water. A beautiful woman, her hair pulled back from her face, bustles around making last minute adjustments to the buffet of food. She looks up and smiles, and you again smile happily. Joy suffuses you, and you realize that you are Home.

You take a seat by the fire, now lit and crackling merrily, and you watch as people come in. Some are lost and move to the quieter corners, not mingling but seemingly a part of the larger group. Others walk around freely, talking with everyone, not staying long in any one place. Still others walk directly to the buffet and never leave, barely pausing in their feasting to thank their hosts before trying some new delicacy. Many people, all beautiful, all wonderful. Mercury greets them all with a smile as they enter and a hug as they leave. Hesta moves among them, beaming at their praise of the feast, and speaking gently to those who look lost, coaxing them to come closer to the fire, to have a small bit of food, to join the group.

But the time comes when you know you must leave.

You thank Hesta for Her generosity, and She smiles and speaks a few words to you. You will remember Her words. At the door your hug from Mercury is accompanied by His words. You will remember His words. The path is a little steeper returning, but you gradually emerge from your trance, refreshed and energized.

Thank Mercury and Hesta. Dismiss the elements, thanking them for their guidance. Open the circle and ground any excess energy you may have.

Setting Membership Criteria

Before we go much further, an overview of some fairly basic group dynamic "rules" is in order.

First, choose members who are committed to working with you and learning from you for a particular length of time on a regular basis. You can choose the time frames that work best for your group, but be clear about what they are and be firm. In my coven, we expect our students to work with us for a year and a day, with a daily commitment to doing the work assigned.

Second, try to choose members with a broad variety of experience and backgrounds—both magickal and mundane. Diversity in the group will stimulate discussion and provide a rich learning environment. Our membership is frequently blessed with members in Australia, and their perception of the seasons—and the Sabbats—opposite ours here in the United States. (We'd be rhapsodizing about the first snow-drop of Spring while CloudSword was watching the leaves turn color.) We also learned from our diverse social and economic lifestyles, from Imago the perpetual student, to PraireSong the Navy SEAL.

Third, think about what size a group you are comfortable leading. This issue is a kind of double-edged sword because a group that is too small will have a difficult time supporting itself, and one too large will tend to collapse under its own weight. Some scholars say that eight is the minimum size for a physical group, and size is less of a factor in a cyber group. So, there is no magick number I can give you—you will have to decide for yourself.

Some issues to consider are:

- ◎ What kind of help do you have in leading the coven? The more help you have, the larger the group can be.

- ◎ Keeping the coven small at first, with a plan to grow after a period of time, is a good idea—especially if you expect that the initial group will act as leaders for the expanded group.

- ◎ Small groups tend to foster a feeling of intimacy, but if the energy gets strange—say if two members suddenly clash over a minor issue—it can be harder to recover.

- ◎ Large groups provide a great deal of stimulation, but can make it difficult for everyone to feel as if they are being heard.

- ◎ Be prepared for some of the people you accept to leave. If you have a magick number in mind, such as thirteen, it is unlikely you'll form a group of that size immediately.

Fourth, choose people who are basically stable—psychologically, emotionally, and financially. This does not mean that you should say no to someone who just lost a job, or went through a divorce a year ago. But "excessive baggage" can create problems in a magickal group, and in the early stages it may be too much of an issue for an individual to also be able to support the group dynamic. Listen to your intuition in this matter and follow its guidance.

Fifth, do not invite people to join just because you "have" to, whether because you personally know them or because the group is too small. It's better to be a smaller, happily intimate group than a larger troubled one. If you are in doubt about someone, do not invite them.

Sixth, I recommend setting a time, perhaps at the end of three months, to ask each member to check in with you about how well the coven is working. Some members may have realized that this is not what they should be doing right now; for others it may be too much work. I would recommend that you release anyone who feels burdened. They would be welcome to return at a future time, but you both will be relieved (them of trying to "keep up," you of "nagging"). Try to keep your early work rich in intensity, but moderate in its time commitment. Such a pace will give your coven a good idea of what is to come, in terms of both learning and in time commitment.

ShadowMoon had many members begin their year who had not thought about the time required to do the work. One member asked to be unsubscribed to the list because she was getting too much mail, yet she wanted to remain in the coven. Another member had a physical world emergency take her away from her computer for a month. Both members chose to leave the coven; the latter returned at a later date, when she was able to commit to the work, in a manner similar to that of a teacher's sabbatical.

~Making Contact~

Keeping these general precepts in mind as you screen your applications will help you make an initial yes/no decision. Another way to decide is on the basis of answers to the questions you may want to ask your applicants, some of which you may want to put into your initial advertisement such as their age and knowledge of the Craft.

Suggested Questions to Ask Applicants

I've been screening applicants to my class since 1998, and am rarely surprised at how people turn out (and when I am, it's a pleasant surprise!). Part of this comes from our refined and modified application and screening process. We don't accept everyone who applies, we are only open to new students once a year, and we are clear that the level of work done by students is similar to that of a graduate-level seminar. (A copy of our current application questionnaire is in Appendix A: Art of Ritual Class Application.)

At a minimum, you want to know what the applicant has done already, with whom (you'll probably want to check this, if you can), and whether her/his lifestyle allows for work with your group. This is the place to check if your applicant has some hidden potential landmines and bring them into the light. For example, take a person who has trained with many people or in many systems. Is s/he unsuited for deeper level work? A "degree collector"? Or perhaps still looking for a system that "fits"? Another example is a person going through a major life change: divorce, moving a home, having a child, or one who lacks basic support systems (no regular employment/schooling, a partner of a violently opposed belief system, and so forth).

I also suggest that you ask why they want to work with you. How did they hear about you/your group? What appealed? What do they expect? What do they offer? That last might sound crude, or off-putting, but remember that you are looking for people to fit within your framework, and they should have something to offer that is unique (having four of six members be accomplished Web designers is asking for trouble, for example).

These questions will help you gather a great deal of information, perhaps more than you need. Select the questions that seem the most appropriate. You may also be interested in asking more questions than I have listed here. For example, a Celtic background or craft knowledge may be particularly desirable for you. Or perhaps you wish to find someone experienced in herbs because you have a black thumb and cannot tell ragweed from rose. You may wish to have others helping you decide whom to accept for membership. As always, use your intuition to guide you in your choice of coven members. If you are unsure about someone, for whatever reason, bring magick into the discussion. Use dreaming, pendulum questioning, or even runes to help the intuitive power at your command speak clearly. Spelling is not an area I would force, however, because if it is right for you to do at this time, the elements will all come together smoothly. I created the following meditation to assist you in tapping your intuitive abilities.

The Dragonfly's Pool

Here is a ritual that will help you tap the power of your intuition:

Cleanse your self and your sacred space. Call the quarters focusing on air's inspiration and new beginnings, fire's energy, water's intuitive link to the psychic realm, and earth's ability to reveal secrets.

Invoke the Lord and Lady and ask Their assistance in strengthening your intuitive ability.

Relax and get comfortable. Close your eyes and take three deep breaths.

The day is overcast, and you are standing near a forest of coniferous trees. There is a wide stream that runs into the wood, and you stand on its bank, looking down into a ravine shaded by ferns and long, dripping moss. You begin your journey, traveling along the stream bank, climbing over fallen logs covered with moss, heavy and dark like velvet.

Bird calls echo around you, and the damp chill smell of autumn is in the air, hinting at the cold nights to come. Gradually the slope of the wood lowers to where you are only a few feet above the stream, and you can see clearly below the surface of the water if you bend down. As you have been walking, the water has been getting deeper and slower, until the surface is like glass.

A dragonfly hovers over the surface of the water—quicksilver, almost as if it is not even there. Its wings are like radiant jewels in the setting sun's light, and the last shards of daylight are glistening on the water before you. It sparkles, reflecting brilliant sapphire, dazzling your eyes. Blind for a moment, you step forward….

You are on the shores of a small grotto. You see crystals glistening in the sand, and the full moon hangs low overhead, casting its light across the mouth of the cave. You stand there for what seems like an utterly timeless moment, transfixed by the beauty you behold.

Gradually you become aware that you are not alone. To one side of the grotto there is a smooth carved hollow. Within that hollow sits a ring of women, beautiful and ethereal. They almost seem like shapes formed of mist. They are singing.

In the center of their midst there is a great throne made of mother of pearl and amethyst, and on the throne a woman cloaked in long streams of dripping seaweed. Her hair is the color of twilight, and she wears a gown woven of fog and raindrops. She sits in front of a large bowl, so large you could almost crawl into it, and in the bowl you see water darker than any water you've ever seen before. She motions for you to come forward.

~Magickal Connections~

When you are standing at her feet, She says, "I am the Queen of Cups, the Queen of Water. You have come to seek my element." Her voice echoes with the roar of the waterfall. She continues, "Know this, I am the force of your body, I am the home from whence life began. Your ancestors swam in my primordial seas. I cushion your tears and soothe you with my gentle raindrops. But I am also the force of the gale, the wild cresting waves. Do not underestimate me, or deny my strength."

She points to the bowl in front of her. "I give you a gift. If you drink from my dark wine while asking a question, then close your eyes. You will hear the answer within your own heart. For my waters unlock the gates to your subconscious, and from there most answers spring." She hands you a crystal goblet and says, "Think of your need to know, then drink and listen for the answer."

When you have finished, She gives you the goblet to keep and says, "Place water that has been charged under the dark moon in this goblet and you may touch the wells of knowledge by drinking deep."

"Go now with my blessing," She says, and pushes you backward into the water.

The shock of it courses through you and you shudder for a moment, nearly dropping the crystal goblet. Recovering, you swim upwards, towards the moon's light. It takes more time than you thought, and when you emerge you tread water, catching your breath. Climbing out onto the shore you rest again.

You are on the shores of shallow stream, holding a crystal goblet in your hand. You take a deep breath, and then another. You open your eyes, refreshed and energized.

Thank the Lord and Lady for Their guidance and care throughout your journey. Dismiss the elements, thanking them for their protection. Open the circle and ground any excess energy you may have.

CHAPTER 3

LEADERSHIP: REALITY CHECK

Your vision will become clear only when you can look into your own heart. Who looks outside, only dreams; who looks inside, also awakens.

—Carl Jung

The job description for a magickal group leader might read as follows: "Leader needed to train a group of people in the mysteries of magick and Divinity. Must have extensive personal knowledge and a desire to work long hours for no financial rewards. Teaching ability, counseling skills, intimate understanding of energy patterns and fluctuations as well as a calm demeanor in tense circumstances are minimum requirements." Yet despite the difficulties, many people believe that the ultimate title within a magickal system is that of High Priest/ess. I agree that there is a certain mystique in being called "Lady X" or "Lord Y," and some respect is accorded to you simply because you claim that title. The reality is that you work very hard, with little (if any) external validation. But if you feel the Call to lead a magickal group for the first time, I understand and respect that Call— no matter what your reason.

~Magickal Connections~

Your reason is important, however. The first step in the creation of a magickal group is self-examination or revelation. Leading does not require that you hold Degrees and have decades of magickal training, although that may help you cope with issues that arise. Instead, the desire to lead is more of an issue of being very clear about what you want to see the magickal group do, and where you hope to see it go. Progressing through the Degrees available in a hierarchical magickal group is usually a reliable, but slow, way of gaining the knowledge necessary to lead, but it is not the only way. There are many ways to run a group, and many different kinds of group structures models, as we saw in Chapter 1.

Presuming that you are the leader, your goals for the group are crucial. To grow with smoothness and strength, the purpose must be clear and the intent must be explicit to incoming members. People self-select based on the information you are giving them. Sometimes that selection will happen after they have already joined, and come to know the members better, but forming a group that remains stable in its membership is a sign of a healthy magickal group.

Motivation Worksheet

THE FOLLOWING QUESTIONS, ANSWERED HONESTLY, WILL HELP YOU DECIDE WHETHER BEING A HIGH PRIEST/ESS AND LEADING A MAGICKAL GROUP IS YOUR VOCATION. I RECOMMEND ANSWERING THEM PERIODICALLY: BEFORE STARTING, AFTER A YEAR, AFTER FIVE YEARS, AND WHEN YOU FEEL "BURNT OUT."

- What is your basic motivation for doing this?
- What are your skills?
- What is your level of commitment? [How much of your life are you willing to commit?]

~Leadership: Reality Check~

◉ What kind of satisfaction are you expecting? (What's your reward?)

◉ What information will you transmit?

◉ What is the group's core purpose? Its secondary purpose(s)?

◉ What are the group's goals?

Hearing the "Call"

I use the word *calling* in an attempt to evoke the sense that being a High Priest/ess is not a job but a vocation, a calling from the God/dess. Are you hearing Her voice or has He shown you this path? If not, it may be your ego, prompting you to take on the mantle of leadership. Leading a spiritual group is not about power, respect, or authority. In the end, it is only about Her and Him.

A friend online described her call:[1]

> One evening, while sitting in a living room surrounded by my magickal group, my Matron Goddess appeared in such a way to me that there was no doubt, and from that moment on, I knew I had to serve Her and be Her priestess. To quote Marion Zimmer Bradley in the book *The Mists of Avalon*, "Once you have felt the kiss of the Goddess on your brow, there is no turning back."[2]
>
> It is certainly not about being the biggest muckity-muck, or having the coolest witchy jewelry; for me it is a deep, heartfelt desire to be of service to the Gods. Service comes in many forms, it is being willing and having the desire to do what needs being done. This can be anything from running the ritual to cleaning the toilets. They are both a needed service.

~Magickal Connections~

Sometimes the most profound mystical experiences are found by being willing to be of service. I can give lots of examples of my own life, as I am sure most folks on this list can do as well. As you already know, it is hard to "explain" to a new person, it is something one must experience. When She calls you, you will know it, and be prepared for anything!

If you think that everyone will do your bidding if you are the leader, you are deluded. That may have been true when finding a group to work with was nearly impossible, and a charismatic leader could command blind obedience, but in today's modern times no one just does what you say without asking questions. We are all too smart for that—or should be. Note that this is especially true in a cyber group, when the ability to look a person in the eye and drown them with charisma is removed. Online, if people do not like what the leader is doing, they will first get quiet and then they will go away.

If you think there will be showers of glory raining down upon you, HA! There are moments, brief ones, where a lot of people will tell you how wonderful you are and how much you have helped them. But they are more likely to tell you that what you just did was great and they really enjoyed it, but they have to go now, and *poof* they're gone, off to put the kids to bed, get a glass of water, or take out the garbage. This is not a situation where you will have worshipping masses. And you will not wield power as a minor deity. Frankly, if you're into a religion of magick because it makes you powerful, you have problems beyond the scope of this book. A word to the wise: Remember that all of our magickal power is derived from the Deity. Ego trips rarely please It.

If you think you can do better than your current teacher, or past ones, then maybe you will. You have the advantage of being able to learn from the mistakes they made, but you will make mistakes of your own. How you deal with those mistakes will be up to you. You are, ultimately, responsible for everything.

One big mistake would be to assume that you will have help. Even when you create a structure to support you in the magickal group mundane life will intervene at the worst possible moment, and you will have to bear a large part of the burden yourself. There is no glory in this job, and you will be lucky if you are thanked for your efforts.

Another mistake you could make would be to assume that you will have to do it alone. People are naturally drawn to roles and every group has a structure—even if it is freeform in nature. You may lead, but you will find yourself complaining or letting off steam to one person, there will be another who always flatters you, one who makes you laugh, and still another who always seems to disagrees with you, challenging your authority. Recognizing who is playing what role will help you do a great job. Allowing those roles to change will help them become better people.

Transmitting Data

It is important that you feel comfortable with the knowledge and wisdom that you have accumulated. As well, you should be clear about how you will transmit that knowledge to the other members of the magickal group. Before we go much further, I must say this: If you truly wish to lead, then I strongly recommend you join an existing group first. Spend a few years being trained and watching group dynamics in action rather than just starting a group from scratch. There are many subtleties of running a strong magickal group that are better seen than read to be understood.

In any magickal group, being a High Priest/ess requires a combination of leadership, administration, teaching, counseling, and group facilitation; think of it as the entire faculty of a high

~Magickal Connections~

school rolled into one person. Most people are very good in some of those areas and can manage in others and may be woefully lacking in still others. You do not have to excel in each of these five areas, but, at a minimum, you want to recognize where you are lacking and look for others who will balance that weakness. Understanding how each of those roles operates in a magickal group is important for any would-be High Priest/ess to know.

Ritual Leadership

Although as the High Priest/ess you should be able to write a good ritual, there is a large gap between writing and leading. As the leader, your magickal group will look to you first for guidance about how to prepare for and perform ritual, as well as how to deal with any unpleasant side effects that may arise. Your purpose and ethics should be clear so that all who enter the circle with you feel safe in doing so; otherwise the group's positive energy will suffer. You should be aware of the nice-ties of timing, especially in a cyber coven where some members will be in different time zones: when to hold a ritual, what time, and how the ritual corresponds with the Moon, the Seasons, and the Zodiac. Perhaps the most slippery skill to have is the understanding of how the energy is flowing within the circle. The energies raised by a magickal group can be enormous and, if the High Priest/ess does not understand what s/he is doing, fails to see it rise, or know when to release it, the resulting situation can grow to be unhealthy.

Group Administration

Completely different from leading is the valuable skill of administration—frequently the area that people have the hardest time doing well. After all, you likely heard your Call based on the strength of your spiritual life. It is a lucky coincidence if you are also a strong administrator. Aside from dividing up the work that needs to be done and then

54

making sure it gets done; checking that the information needed is available (calendars, messages, telephone calls, and so on); and making sure that accurate records are kept (attendance, finances, and so forth), administration frequently encompasses the "downside" of a magickal group: cajoling and chastising people to do what needs to be done. Even in the most freeform of magickal groups, someone is usually keeping track of what needs to be and is being done (if only haphazardously).

Teaching

Teaching is vital, even if you have not created a teaching group. When you are the High Priest/ess, the knowledge you share, or allow to be shared, is the same as if you were actively teaching that information. As a result, information sharing of any nature requires your supervision. Pay attention to whether the information is given in a genuine and respectful manner. This information should allow all participants to ask questions to clarify their understanding or concerns. Does it support your group's goals and purposes? Is it ethical? Magick is a powerful tool and your position as High Priest/ess requires that you safeguard its use.

Counseling

Aside from doing magick, counseling may be the most important aspect of the High Priest/ess's role. You will be expected to help your group members with many personal problems, working with them to find solutions or coping mechanisms. Having the capacity to listen without judgment, a high degree of empathy, the ability to think clearly about emotional situations, personal experience, and some degree of insight are skills that will help you deal with these situations. A degree in psychology or social work is not necessary, but you may find it invaluable to at least do some reading in the subject area, if only to know when it is time to direct the member to another resource.[3] It is not always wise to solve a problem—especially if there is a specific lesson to be learned. Reminding the member to allow the problem to exist—to trust that it is necessary—takes a great deal of courage, but such a reminder can be the best solution of all.

One thing that you will often be asked is to give magickal advice. In part, that means that you'll be asked: "Should I do this spell?" or "Am I the victim of negative magick?" Such requests mean that you will want to recommend solutions that are not "logical" to members who come to you for help. This can include spending extra time meditating upon the problem or exploring recent dreams with them in an effort to find an appropriate solution. You may help them create a ritual specifically designed to solve the problem, or to ask for further understanding of the situation. They may be looking for a "quick fix," but your duty as High Priest/ess is to encourage their growth and learning. It may take longer than expected.

Facilitating

Facilitating the group is the last "hat" the High Priest/ess wears. Group dynamics can be tricky, especially online, where visual cues are lacking. To succeed in this role, I suggest that you be familiar with guiding discussions to keep them flowing, moving toward a decision, while also making sure that everyone is heard. Particularly important skills would be in conflict resolution and closure, and this book has many suggestions for developing your skills.[4]

This may be lighting a bonfire, but it is not necessary to be initiated to the Third Degree (or an equivalent high-level title) to lead a magickal group. Many traditions allow you to lead (usually under supervision of some sort) after the Second Degree (or non-Wiccan equivalent), and if you have been practicing solitary, then you can call yourself whatever you want. It is probably helpful to have at least belonged to a magickal group at some point in your magickal career, because it is hard to lead a magickal group if you have never participated in one. It is akin to being the owner of a jazz music store if you have never listened to jazz or a teacher without ever being a student. Possible, but difficult.

Leadership Roles Exercise

THIS EXERCISE REQUIRES A GREAT DEAL OF HONESTY, BUT IS A WONDERFULLY VISUAL WAY OF SEEING YOURSELF.

GATHER TOGETHER A VARIETY OF COLORED PENS, PENCILS, OR OTHER WRITING MATERIALS, AND A BLANK SHEET OF PAPER. LIGHT A CANDLE AND SOME MEDITATIVE INCENSE.

ON THE PAPER, DRAW A LARGE CIRCLE, AND THEN DIVIDE IT INTO FIVE SECTIONS. AROUND THE EDGES, LABEL THE FIVE SECTIONS: LEADERSHIP, ADMINISTRATION, TEACHING, COUNSELING, AND FACILITATING. NOW COLOR EACH AREA LIGHTER OR DARKER ACCORDING TO HOW WEAK OR STRONG YOU FEEL IN THAT AREA.

WHEN FINISHED, CONTEMPLATE THE MANDALA OF YOUR SKILLS. LOOK FOR PATTERNS INDICATING AREAS WHERE YOU NEED HELP. WRITE NOTES, QUESTIONS, CONCERNS, AND COMMENTS WHERE APPROPRIATE. OFTENTIMES THE FORM THAT HELP WOULD BEST COME IN IS CLEAR. THERE MIGHT BE ANOTHER PERSON WITH SKILLS BETTER THAN YOUR OWN IN SOME AREAS, OR A CLASS TO TAKE TO EXPAND YOUR SKILLS. IN ANY CASE, YOU WILL WANT TO LOOK FOR THE RESOURCES TO BRING YOU THE KNOWLEDGE AND SKILLS YOU NEED.

TAKE ACTION ON THE INFORMATION THIS EXERCISE HAS BROUGHT YOU.

Your Commitment, Your Reward

If you see yourself involved in every aspect of the group, you will probably get tired very quickly. There are many ways to lead, even if others facilitate meetings, lead rituals, and so forth. You could be the founder, easing into the background over time, your title one of respect and honor. Perhaps you are most comfortable being the center of the group, without which it fails. Or you only want to write and lead rituals. Then again, there are many roles in between. As the founder, you have a great deal of authority, and deciding where you wish to bestow that power can be a difficult decision.

You will want to think about how much time you feel is necessary to spend on this project—six months, a year, longer?—and how often you want to work on it. If it takes more time than you expect, where is your "bottom line"? I can guarantee that you will devote more time and energy than you sometimes want to, particularly in the beginning. Be prepared for that eventuality. Having an idea of how much is "too much," and updating it periodically, will keep you focused and strong—two vital qualities in a High Priest/ess.

I know there is some kind of reward or particular pleasure you will derive from this endeavor. If not, then stop for a minute and review your motives. Not many of us are so altruistic as to take on a lifetime's work when we do not expect any reward, although what that reward actually is can vary wildly. While you are at it, think about when you would like to start getting positive reinforcement. As well, be clear about what you will do if you are not enjoying yourself, and what you will do if it turns out to be too hard.

Defining the Purpose

Each magickal group has a primary purpose; in some cases it has several. Although both of my covens have been teaching covens, that is not the only model. There are magickal groups that only meet to do rituals, share information, or explore the complexities of magick.[5] Still others act as a social activity, gathering in a community of eclectic celebrations. Some focus on one aspect of the God/dess, such as the Dianic groups who do not recognize the authority of the God in Divine matters.

~Leadership: Reality Check~

Others derive their knowledge from particular mythological sources, or historical periods, such as Celtic Traditionalists.

Your decision as to the magickal group's purpose will define its structure and the nature of the people you choose as members. If it is to be a Wiccan teaching magickal group, you may choose people who have little or no knowledge of Wicca, although they may have been practicing magick for years. If your focus is Celtic magick, your background in that area should be strong and you want to choose people who have an affinity for Celtic traditions. The group could be one in which expanding personal growth is a primary focus, or perhaps one of activists sharing stories, providing support for one another's exploits.

Thinking to the Future

This is perhaps the hardest aspect of planning in the earliest stages of creating a magickal group. If you are going to create a magickal group that lasts longer than a year, you should consider training a successor. Knowing there is a person who is qualified to lead at times when you are unable to do so will ease you of a huge burden. Keeping this in mind in the beginning will allow you to choose magickal group members who have some experience, or a lot, and will support and relieve you when you ask. It will also allow you to think of the future, a positive future, when your magickal group is so large that some members must hive off and go forth into the world. A lovely idea!

Ethical Considerations

In assuming the role of High Priest/ess, you are taking on a responsibility to both past and future Witches. Transmitting information not your own or not directly given to you is a betrayal of that responsibility. The online world has made it easy—too easy in fact—to get information, and oftentimes it belongs to another person. Grabbing it for your personal Book of Shadows is one thing; teaching it, which implies that it is your knowledge directly, is a completely different—and illegal—activity. Is your information old, new, or borrowed (or blue)? Be clear about your sources, your teachers, and your perspective. If you use information from others, do you have permission to pass it on?

Online ethics are somewhat tangled at this time—or, at the very least, mostly unregulated—but that is no excuse to just copy information and pass it off as your own. Common courtesy is the best rule to use when deciding whether or not to use someone else's work to teach a lesson. Put yourself in the author's place: If you made it, would you want other people to use it, and would you want attribution? You may not care if others use the information, but you probably want credit for the effort.

On a non-legal level, make sure the information is in a transmittable format. Once upon a time we hand-copied it from the handwritten books our Elders revealed to us as we progressed through training. I will tell you now that if my covenmates had to do this I'd be practicing solitary, as my handwriting is so bad that *I* have a hard time reading it. There are several options for transmission. If the data is hardcopy, you will probably transcribe it into a text file and send it out via e-mail, depending on how fast you type. If you have images you may want to think about how you would either textually describe them, or invest in a scanner to copy them into your computer and send them out in graphic format.

In becoming a High Priest/ess, you are continuing a tradition that has existed since the world was entirely Pagan. Our world has grown increasingly complex, and the issues our Priestesses face each day have also grown complicated. Your students will reflect your training, your attitudes, and your ego. Whether you like it or not, wish it or not, there will be people who insist the High Priestess lives on a pedestal. It is flattering, yes, but that kind of ego-stroking evaporates in the light of day, when our human frailties are revealed. Never forget that leading is a growth experience for the leader as much as for those following, and *what you are* will profoundly influence your group, far more than anything you will ever say.

For women, leadership can be an especially difficult skill. The world is changing, but generally speaking we play supportive roles in our daily lives (work, home, family). Stepping into the circle as a leader can be a new place for us, an intense experience, and one that really can go to our heads quickly. This is probably the number-one reason for "High Priestess Disease" (when a Priestess gets a little too caught up in the glamour of the role, and loses sight of the responsibilities). Although I feel that this problem will gradually work its way out, and a little humility will go a long way towards the cure, I offer this example to help us keep perspective: In my coven we have a "thwap!" rule. Each member of my coven has absolute license to thwap me if it seems I am getting vain about my contributions. Knowing that I might get thwapped makes me stop and think about what I am saying, and (more importantly) what I am about to do. I don't get thwapped often, and I hate it when it happens, but it has always been a good opportunity for reflection and course correction.

Finally, I offer you a piece from Egyptian Mythology. Called the Holy Laws of Maat, these are the answers to the questions asked of the dead as their souls are weighed against the feather of Truth:

I have not told lies.

I have not committed fraud.

I have not caused anyone to weep.

I have not done violence to anyone.

I have not fouled water.

I have not driven cattle from their pastures.

I have not stolen the property of others.

I have not cheated in the weighing of grain.

I have not forced anyone to do excessive daily work for me.

I have not enriched myself at others' expense.

I have not taken milk from infants.

I have not harmed animals.

I have not robbed the dead.

I have not defiled the sanctuaries.

I have not caused murder to be done.

I have not caused suffering.

I have not offended against the holy laws of Maat.

Asking the God/dess

Although being a witch does not guarantee a high degree of self-awareness, it should. Our perception of our selves and our motivations must be clear because the working of successful magick requires exceptional self-knowledge and focus. As a High Priest/ess, the intimate knowledge of your strengths and weaknesses, as well as those of the magickal group members, is vital to the strength of your magickal group. Your personality is not "cast in stone"; you can modify not only your perception of the world and therefore your responses to it, but also how others see and respond to you. In fact, I assume that all Witches choose to undergo consistent self-examination and modification in order to improve their personal realities.

If you have received formal training and degrees, then you most likely have at least some awareness of your potential and problems. I caution you not to assume your plusses and minuses will remain the same over time, and I urge you to do regular inventories to verify any changes. If you have

~Leadership: Reality Check~

practiced solitary, you may be less sure of your qualities. The rest of this chapter provides you with tools to confirm your abilities. Use this chapter to start your journey, but work hard to expand on the information I have provided here.

Fortunately as witches, we can call upon resources and techniques special to religion—meditations and ritual. Following are a few visualizations designed to increase your self-awareness. They are unusual in their design, but quite powerful.

Visualization: "The Funhouse"

This exercise is vivid and evocative. While sitting comfortably, read or listen to the instructions and respond as images or responses pop into your head. Do not think about it, just answer by writing (or typing).

You are at a carnival, and you enter a funhouse. Do you give the carnie a ticket, coins, or money? Does he just let you on by? What does he look like? Does he seem to be operating any machinery? What is the weather like? What does the entrance and outside look like? Is it a scary funhouse or a silly funhouse?

You walk through the entrance and onto a path with spinning disks. Which way do you spin? Do you get dizzy? Do you simply hop across them onto the stairs?

The stairs take you onto a swinging bridge. Is the bridge rubbery-bouncy, or wood, or metal? Do you swing and bounce? Do you rush across it?

Check the background. Is it colorful? Is it dark? Do you hear music in the background?

At the end of the swinging bridge is a maze of mirrors. Describe yourself in the different distortions you see. Do any of the distortions resemble your actual self-perception? Do you stop and play, or do you head on to the glass maze?

How do you find your way through the maze? Do you figure your way through the optical illusion? Do you use geometry? Do you simply bump your way through it, touching the glass? When you touch the glass, do you leave fingerprints?

At the end of the maze are a fireman's pole, a slide, and some stairs. All lead to the small opening at the end of the house. Which do you take? How does it feel?

You must cross through two openings to make the exit. The first opening is a large, spinning wheel. Do you ride the wheel all the way around, do you tread sideways to get across it, do you hop or somersault over it?

The second is a large doorway that simply rocks back and forth. Do you ride it for a while, do you try to dance on it or toss a penny to see it slide back and forth? Do you just hop down it without gyrating with it?

As you come out of the opening, and at the end of the journey, how does the world look? What does the carnie look like? What does the road look like?

Now, look at your responses. Read them as if you are reading a story. Do you like this character—why or why not? What will you change?[6]

Visualizations for During Ritual

Unlike the Funhouse Meditation, which can be done at any introspective moment, the following three meditations are to be used as a part of ritual. They come from my Book of Shadows, and I have used them over the years to access my own self-knowledge. They are powerful. You may use them as they are written or modify them to suit your own personality.

Before beginning each meditation of the following meditations, cast a protective circle, and invoke the guardian aspects of the four quarters and your particular Deities. I recommend having a journal of some kind with you in your circle, so that you may use the sacred energy you have invoked to help you record the lessons learned on your journey. After you have completed your meditative journey, thank the Deities for their guidance, and the Quarters for their protection. Close the circle and ground any excess energy.

Visualization: Council of Selves

Focus on your breathing; allow it to take you deep into yourself...deeper...deeper still.

You find yourself at the entrance to a mansion. Enter it and begin to walk though the rooms. You see many wonderful things here. Take the time to examine them.

Eventually you find yourself in a round room with a huge round table in the center of it. Moving to the table you call out: "Let the Council begin!" in a loud, ringing voice. Sit down. Many doors appear in the walls and through them come figures, which you recognize. Your Old Wise self, your Merry Child, all of your counseling Selves are there—even the ones you did not know you had. They sit at the table.

Stand again and speak to them of your concerns, your questions. Listen as each one speaks in turn. You are before a powerful Council.

Look at each aspect and thank it for its advice and love and support. When you are finished call out "The Council has ended!" and watch as the room is flooded with light. The aspects leave with the light.

You leave the room, knowing you can return again at any time, and make your way out of the house.

You awaken refreshed and energized.

~Magickal Connections~

Visualization: Hall of Mirrors

Focus on your breathing, allow it to take you deep into yourself...deeper...deeper still.

You find yourself at the entrance to a mansion. Enter it and begin to walk though. You see many wonderful things here. Take the time to examine them.

You find yourself in a long hall; on each wall there are many mirrors. Breathe deeply and look into the first mirror on your right. You see your Self there, the most relevant aspect. Look at this aspect and recognize its characteristics and attributes—you will remember them later.

Breathe deeply and open yourself to its wisdom. When it is finished, thank it for its insight and move to the next mirror.

Continue looking into each mirror in the hall, taking your time, breathing deeply and calmly as you absorb the knowledge and wisdom of all of your Aspects. As you finish with each aspect, thank it for its advice.

When you are finished, take a deep breath and bow low in respect to the Hall of Mirrors. Turn and move back through the house.

You leave the house and return to consciousness, knowing you can return again, as you will.

You are relaxed and energized.

Visualization: Wise Old Woman

Focus on your breathing, allow it to take you deep into yourself...deeper...deeper still.

Within the sea of images and archetypes is a wise old woman. She lives deeply within you. You see her below you and you swim down. You are heavy and strong, moving towards her until you stand before her.

~Leadership: Reality Check~

She greets you and welcomes you to her realm. You remain with her, listening to her wisdom and asking questions of her.

Thank her for her advice and assistance. Promise to do something to honor her when you return to the waking world. Tell her what you will do. She smiles in pleasure at being honored in such a way.

Slowly, then faster you gradually swim back through the sea of images, upwards, growing lighter. Move upward until you begin to return to the waking world. You awaken, refreshed and filled with energy.

Open your eyes and record the knowledge you gained.

Visualization: Stage Door

Relax, deepen, and calm yourself.

You are fully relaxed and you begin to walk. You travel through a variety of landscapes until you come upon a theatre.

You enter, moving through the lobby to the auditorium. The lights are dim and there is no one there. You take a seat and the lights go dim.

The curtain lifts and you watch yourself—you are the star of this play! You see yourself, all of your selves, acting in their own unique way. Your angry self, your sad self, your generous self—all of your selves are there—even ones you did not know you had.

One by one they appear before you, revealing their nature to you. You are open to their messages and listen eagerly to their wisdom. Listen to them now. The curtain falls as the last self finishes. You may return here at any time to see how they have changed. You rise, stretch and walk through the auditorium, then into the lobby and outside.

You return, walking slowly through the landscapes, continuing to savor the wisdom given to you.

You awake fully refreshed and energized.

CHAPTER 4

BECOMING A LEADER

With rare exceptions, good leaders are made, not born. In some cases a person is nominated to leadership by popular acclaim, but in spiritual circles the role usually comes as part of the "Call" from the God/dess. For many of us, the Call comes when we are feeling unprepared to lead, but if we have the desire and willpower, we can develop our ability and become effective leaders. It is a never-ending process of self-study, education, training, and experience—no resting on our laurels for us!

Before we go further, let's define leadership. One definition is that it is a process by which a person influences others to accomplish an objective and directs the group in a way that makes it more cohesive and coherent. Leaders carry out this process by applying their beliefs, values, ethics, knowledge, and skills. Although we may already have the authority to accomplish certain tasks and objectives in our group, this power does not make us a leader; it simply makes us the boss. A leader is different from a boss in that s/he makes the followers want to achieve high goals, rather than simply doing what they are told.

~Magickal Connections~

There are three basic ways to explain how people become leaders:[1]

◉ Having personality traits that guide them naturally into leadership roles (Trait Theory).

◉ Experiencing a crisis or important event that brings out hitherto unknown leadership qualities in an otherwise ordinary person (Great Events Theory).

◉ Choosing to acquire leadership skills through education (Transformational Leadership Theory).

When a person is deciding if s/he respects you as a leader, s/he probably isn't thinking about your attributes, but instead relies on observation. This reveals whether you are honorable and can be trusted as a leader—or are a self serving person who misuses authority to look good and receive undue accolades. Ironically, a self serving leader can still be effective for a period of time.

The basis of good leadership is honorable character and selfless service to your group. To other members, your leadership is everything you do that effects the group's objectives and the individuals' well being. Respected leaders concentrate on what they are (such as beliefs and character), what they know (such as skills, tasks, and human nature), and what they do (such as implementing new projects, motivating group members, and providing direction). People want to be guided by those they respect and who have a clear sense of direction. Therefore, the most important skills as a leader are the ability to be trustworthy and to communicate the vision of where the group needs to go.

How do you achieve maximum ability with these skills?

1. **Know yourself, and seek continual self-improvement.** Seeking self-improvement means constantly strengthening your abilities through study, self-reflection, and interacting with others.

2. **Be technically proficient.** As a leader, you must know your job and have a solid familiarity with every task those around you are doing. (This does not mean you have to be able to do it, just that you know how it is supposed to be done.)

3. **Take responsibility for your actions.** When things go wrong (as they always do sooner or later) do not blame others. Analyze the situation, take corrective action, and move on to the next challenge.

4. **Make sound decisions.** Use good problem-solving, decision-making, and planning tools.

5. **Be the example.** Be a good role model for your group members. They must not only hear what they are expected to do, but also see.

6. **Keep the group informed.** Know how to communicate with them, rather than dictate.

7. **Develop a sense of responsibility in others.** Help them develop their abilities as leaders as well as their responsibilities to themselves.

Leadership Styles

Every leader has a manner of providing direction, implementing plans, and motivating people. Good leaders tend to use more than one, depending on the circumstance, but there will be a "baseline" from which s/he operates. Kurt Lewin and colleagues did leadership decision experiments in 1939 and identified three different styles of leadership, in particular around decision-making:[2]

1. Authoritarian (most commonly seen when the group's structure is based on the triangle).

2. Participative (most often seen in circle structures).

◉ Free Reign (most often seen in freeform groups).

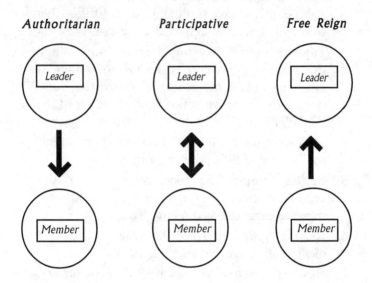

Authoritarian (Autocratic)

The authoritarian style is that of the sergeant at arms. This is the "do this, do that, and get it done now" method, and the leader rarely asks for advice or input from group members. It is ideal for getting things done quickly, when the leader already has the information needed to make the best decision (or is perhaps the only person qualified to answer the question) and group members are motivated.

Despite my use of the military image, being autocratic does not mean that yelling, putting people down, or making threats is usual. That is a bully's version—the dark side of an otherwise useful way to deal with specific occasions. The authoritarian style should only be used on rare occasions as it will encourage a culture of following and dependence.

~Becoming a Leader~

A subgroup of the authoritarian leader is the **charismatic** leader. This type of leader gathers followers by exerting charm, rather than exercising any form of external power or authority. S/he may engender trust through visible self-sacrifice and taking personal risks in the name of her/his beliefs and will often show great confidence in specific followers. Charismatic leaders tend to be very persuasive and often effectively use body language as well as verbal language. Many politicians use a charismatic style, as they need to gather a large number of followers. Religious leaders, too, may well use charisma, as do cult leaders.

Charismatic leaders who are building a group will often focus on making the group very distinct from other groups. They then build the image of the group as being far superior to all others. This leader will typically attach him- or herself firmly to the identity of the group, such that to join the group is to become one with the leader. In doing so, he/she creates an unchallengeable position for himself/herself.

Participative (Democratic)

The participative style is that of the diplomat. Here, the leader includes one or more members in the decision-making process. Usually, the leader retains the final decision making authority. This is the best style to use when the leader has part of the information, but not all, and other members likely have the other parts. This can be an ideal style because it is of mutual benefit: It allows members to better understand your role, increases their sense of participation, and provides the leader with better information with which to make decisions. It can run into trouble when the leader asks for too much information, or doesn't like the advice given. It can also be slow (and is, particularly in comparison with the authoritarian style).

~Magickal Connections~

A sub-type of the participative leader is the **transformational** leader. This type of leader starts with a vision (often radical) that excites and converts potential followers. The leader then "sells" the vision, using every opportunity to convince others to climb on board the bandwagon. Transformational leaders are very careful about creating trust, and their personal integrity is a critical part of the package that they are selling. In effect, they are selling themselves as well as the vision.

Overall, this leader balances his/her attention between action that creates progress and the mental happiness of his/her followers. Perhaps more than other approaches, these leaders are people-oriented and believe that success comes first and last through deep and sustained commitment. Their vision may be outward-directed (change the world!) but carries a tacit promise to followers that they also will be transformed in some way, perhaps to be more similar to this amazing leader. In some respects, then, the followers are the product of the transformation.

One of the traps of transformational leadership is that passion and confidence can easily be mistaken for truth and reality. Although it is true that great things have been achieved through enthusiastic leadership, it is also true that many passionate people have led the charge right over the cliff and into a bottomless chasm. Just because someone believes s/he is right, does not mean that s/he is right.

Another sub-type is the **quiet** leader. This type of leader is the antithesis of both the charismatic and transformational leaders. Quiet leaders base their success on actions and, to a lesser degree, their thoughts. They are strongly task-focused and tend to persuade people through rational argument and a form of benevolent dictatorship.

An example of the quiet leader comes from the Taoist writings of Lao Tzu's *Tao Te Ching*. Tzu described this leader as barely known, trusting and trusted, action-oriented without unnecessary speech, and virtually invisible.

For people accustomed to an extraverted charismatic style, a quiet style can be very confusing, and they may downplay the person, which is usually a mistake. Successful quiet leaders often invoke values to persuade others. The difficulty here is when the group falls into a pattern of "peace at all costs" and any form of conflict or challenge is discouraged.

Free Reign (Delegative)

The free reign leader allows (and encourages) group members to make decisions. This is an ideal situation when members are able to analyze the situation and determine what needs to be done and how to do it. It is a difficult style to manifest in most situations as it requires the full trust and confidence in the members.

A sub-type of the free reign leader is the **servant** leader, increasingly found in non-profit and religious organizations. Here, leadership is based upon the premise that s/he who leads, serves. By assisting others to achieve and improve (and, ultimately, become servant leaders themselves) the servant leader fulfills her/his role.

This role is aligned with the transformational leader in that personal growth and evolution is encouraged. As does the quiet leader, however, the servant uses collaboration and commitment as the basic decision-making process. The servant leader uses community-building to create environments of trust and frequently focuses on nurturing the spirit.

An example of a servant leader is Ernest Shackleton, the early-20th-century explorer who, after his ship became frozen in the Antarctic, brought every one of his 27-member crew home alive, a trip that included an 800-mile journey in open boats across the winter Antarctic seas. It took two years, but

~Magickal Connections~

Shackleton's sense of responsibility towards his men never wavered.

Servant leadership is a morality-based role, one in which the well being of the followers is more important than other goals. It is a natural model for working in the public sector (balancing the needs of the "bottom line" against individual well-being is usually too stressful to accomplish).

The trap for this style of leader is the assumption that the followers want to change, and to what degree or in what manner. As well, there is the difficult question of just what "better" is, and who decides what makes it better.

Leadership Style Assessment

ANSWER THE FOLLOWING QUESTIONS WITH **ALWAYS, OFTEN, SOMETIMES,** OR **NEVER,** GOING WITH YOUR FIRST RESPONSE. KEEP IN MIND THAT THERE IS NO RIGHT ANSWER, JUST INDICATIONS OF YOUR PERSONAL STYLE.

AS A LEADER, I TEND TO...

1. MAKE MY OWN DECISIONS.
2. TELL OTHERS WHAT TO DO.
3. SUGGEST A DECISION TO OTHERS.
4. PERSUADE OTHERS TO DO THINGS MY WAY.
5. PARTICIPATE EQUALLY.
6. PROVIDE RESOURCES TO OTHERS.
7. GATHER FEEDBACK BEFORE DECIDING.
8. RELY ON MY OWN JUDGMENT.
9. MAKE SURE THE MAJORITY RULES.
10. TURN DECISION OVER TO OTHERS.
11. ASK OTHERS TO BRAINSTORM CHOICES.
12. SHARE MY OWN IDEAS.

~Becoming a Leader~

NOW, ASSIGN NUMBERS TO THE ANSWERS: ALWAYS = 4, OFTEN = 3, SOMETIMES = 2, AND NEVER = 1. ADD THE NUMBERS TOGETHER FOR THE FOLLOWING GROUPS OF QUESTIONS:

QUESTIONS 1, 2, 4, 8   _____AUTOCRATIC

QUESTIONS 3, 7, 9, 11   _____PARTICIPATORY

QUESTIONS 5, 6, 10, 12   _____FREE REIGN

Good leaders use a combination of all styles, changing modes as the situation requires it. Some examples include:

- Using an authoritarian style when starting a new group. Perhaps relying on a charismatic person to reach out to new members and provide the "vision."

- Switching to a participative mode after the group has settled. Here, the Transformational leader begins to assess the deeper needs of the group members and moves to create solutions.

- Transforming the group into one where the Servant leader manifests, creating a culture of deep reverence for positive personal transformation.

A sign of an inexperienced leader (or a bad one) is a tendency to stick with one style.

CHAPTER 5

BASIC GROUP DYNAMICS

Community.
Somewhere there are people to whom we can speak with
passion without having the words catch in our throats.
Somewhere a circle of hands will open to receive us, eyes
will light up as we enter, voices will celebrate with us when-
ever we come into our own power.... A circle of healing. A
circle of friends. Somewhere we can be free.

—Starhawk

The fundamental decision to join a magickal group can be
complicated. It may involve a desire for social interaction or
education, or offer the opportunity for boosting one's ego. I
see the formation of a magickal group as one that involves
three factors: making a connection, building the Group mind,
and maintaining clear energy between group members.

~Magickal Connections~

Making Connections

People looking for community are looking for an intimate, warm, friendly group of people similar to themselves, one small enough that everyone knows everyone else, but large enough to keep fresh perspectives flowing. Being a member of any community, whether it is a church, a school, or your neighborhood, often depends less on the group and more on what you do in it. As the leader of a cyber coven, one of the most common questions I am asked is: How connected to one another do members feel? The answer is that the sense of connection is dependent upon the interaction the member engages in; the same is true for physical group—which is to say that the energy put into a group dynamic is what is returned in greater measure.

Magickal groups meet as their schedules allow: monthly, weekly, or perhaps only to celebrate the seasonal rituals. In between, members may spend time socializing with one another, increasing their connections to each other. In some groups this is enough to create a sense of unity so that magickal workings are clear, focused, and direct. In other groups there may still be a sense of not "jelling" or coming together, in which case magickal workings are not as powerful. In my experience, magickal groups with a greater sense of unity most likely spend time sharing personal information and working with group energy at each meeting.

There are a variety of exercises that a magickal group might use when adding new members or when getting started. The focus is on fun and getting to know one another, although some exercises will informally help the High Priest/ess gauge each member's level of magickal knowledge and perceptions. If this were a business setting, you might call them icebreakers. These exercises and others along the same lines allow members to become more than just the person who sits in the same room as us, or text on a screen—the answers make us flesh, real. We learn about our self-perceptions, our desires, and our frustrations. We tell stories to one another, in an environment in which we know that our words will be paid attention to, read by all, and kept "forever" in the memory of our archives. There is a powerful magick in telling a story, and having it heard by an audience, knowing you have imparted a piece of yourself to another. The day I found the courage to share a piece of bad news with my class is a special memory for me. I had been let go from my work, a move that came as a complete surprise to me, and the first time a decision to leave a job did not happen as a result of my desire. I was devastated and, for a moment, hesitated to tell my group. Instead, I gathered my courage and shared my fear, my anger, and my feeling of being lost. Their response? Loving support and a welcome place to share my woes. Several members later told me that my sharing with them made me more human and approachable.

Every group has a core, a sacred center that is invisible and intangible. Nonetheless it is the heart around which we revolve, to which we move and from which we turn, constantly reforming and reevaluating our relationships with the others in the group and with our selves.

IF GROUP MEMBERS SHARE E-MAIL, THESE ARE GREAT TOPICS AND EXERCISES TO DO TO INCREASE THE FEELING OF CONNECTION TO ONE ANOTHER.

DAILY Q&AS

EACH DAY (OR EVERY FEW DAYS) MEMBERS TAKE A TURN AT POSTING A QUESTION FOR DISCUSSION. HERE ARE SOME TOPICS TO EXPLORE:

◎ *WHAT IS MAGICK?*

◎ *WHEN HAVE YOU DONE MAGICK? WAS IT DELIBERATE OR ACCIDENTAL? HOW DID IT MAKE YOU FEEL?*

~Magickal Connections~

- WHAT IS THE SINGLE MOST IMPORTANT BENEFIT OF MAGICK?
- WHAT DO YOU THINK IT MEANS TO BE A WITCH?
- WHAT DOES THE ABILITY TO USE MAGICK MEAN TO YOU PERSONALLY?

Daily Meds

EACH MEMBER OF THE GROUP TAKES A TURN, FOR A WEEK AT A TIME, POSTING A FILE (A PIECE OF TEXT, AN IMAGE, OR EVEN MUSIC). THESE FILES FOCUS OUR ATTENTION UPON A SINGLE IDEA AS WE VIEW IT AND PERHAPS DISCUSS IT. THIS CREATES A CONSTANT FLOW OF ENERGY MOVING AROUND THE WORLD, NEVER CEASING, AND INCREASING IN STRENGTH WITH EACH NEW DAY.

The Magick Wand

YOU JUST FOUND A MAGICK WAND THAT ALLOWS YOU TO CHANGE ANYTHING YOU WANT TO IN THREE ASPECTS OF YOUR LIFE. HOW (AND WHAT) WOULD YOU CHANGE? DISCUSS WHY IT IS IMPORTANT TO MAKE THE CHANGE. A VARIATION IS TO DISCUSS WHAT YOU WOULD CHANGE IF YOU BECAME A GOD/DESS FOR A WEEK.

Marooned

YOU ARE MAROONED ON AN ISLAND. WHAT FIVE ITEMS WOULD YOU HAVE BROUGHT WITH YOU IF YOU KNEW THERE WAS A CHANCE THAT YOU MIGHT BE STRANDED? SHARE YOUR ITEMS, AND WHY.

The Interview

BREAK THE GROUP INTO PAIRS. HAVE EACH PAIR INTERVIEW EACH OTHER OVER A SET PERIOD OF TIME. THEY NEED TO LEARN ABOUT WHAT EACH OTHER LIKES ABOUT THEIR JOB, PAST JOBS, FAMILY LIFE, HOBBIES, FAVORITE SPORT, AND SO ON. AFTER THE TIME IS UP, HAVE EACH INTRODUCE THE OTHER TO THE GROUP.

Energy Work

Another basic skill for magickal groups is to understand how their energy flows from one another—specifically, how the energy flows effect the chakras, the seven core energetic centers of the physical body. The scope of this topic can fill an entire book,[1] so I can only give you a basic overview and guide-lines. At the least, understanding and being aware of one's own energy patterns is extremely important before leading a group's energy in ritual.

The concept of chakras came to Western awareness from India, and the word is *Sanskrit*, meaning "wheel." Chakras may be described as swirling vortexes, flowers, or balls of light, each of which corresponds to a different color, number, tone, and part of the body. Energy is pulled into the body through the chakras and distributed along the spine so that it flows throughout the entire body in an even pattern. When each chakra is open and the body is in balance the flow of energy is also balanced and energizing, and when there are blockages or closures, difficulties and imbalance arise.

When doing energy work with others, that energy will affect each person to a small degree, but it can strongly affect the leader, who is the focus of that energy, directing it and manipulating it towards the group's desired goal. Keeping your chakras clear and paying attention to imbalances immediately is therefore a necessary part of leading a magickal group.

There are many systems of understanding the charkas; I use one in which there are seven:

Name	Color	Location
Base	Red	Base of the spine
Belly	Orange	About 2 inches below the belly button
Solar Plexus	Yellow	At the diaphragm
Heart	Green	Between the pectorals
Throat	Blue	In the hollow where the throat meets the chest
Third eye	Purple	Middle of the forehead
Crown	White	Top of the head

~Magickal Connections~

Each chakra is associated with different properties, including food, psychological issues, stones, herbs, and animals. We are (generally speaking) taller than we are wide, and so the energy flows between the chakras in an up-down-up motion. If there is an over-stimulation or lack of energy in a particular area of one's life, then the chakra will be too open or closed to properly apply the energy drawn into the corresponding chakra.

THE SEVEN CHAKRAS.

A deficient chakra is one in which the energy flow is restricted more than is comfortable. (Imagine a valve being too small to allow water to flow freely through it.) New stimulations cannot be accepted through a restricted chakra; it is blocked. This means that whatever activities associated with that chakra (sexual feelings, emotions, communication) are also blocked. Reactions to others are muted or non-existant. There may even be physical manifestations as a result (such as a sore throat or little interest in sexual activities).

~Basic Group Dynamics~

In the case where a chakra is too wide open (commonly referred to as excessive) the wide opening permits extraneous energy or emotions to be collected there, blocking the internal energy from emerging. Here we see great imbalance within a person, and although reactions to others are present, they are frequently not proportionate to the situation. For example, an excessive fifth chakra (throat) may result in someone talking far too much and dominating the conversation. Or an excessive first chakra may manifest as the need to possess objects, food, or money.

Being aware of your own energy levels and patterns is another skill the well-trained Pagan is to learn and maintain. These cycles will vary, of course, throughout one's lifetime, but certain elements are more likely than not to be constant. I, for example, am much more mentally alert in the morning; some of my best work is done before noon. Also, because I am a Virgo, I find that when the moon is in Pisces each month, I have a very difficult time staying focused and being organized. Those two-to-three days are essentially lost to me, and I have learned over the years to try and keep outside needs to a minimum those times. Seasonally, my most active time is the autumn and the least active is winter. None of this is an absolute, but a general pattern that helps me to navigate my life.

Your energy is the most important, in any circumstance, normally speaking, and paying attention to it will benefit you in many ways. In a group, knowing how your energy is flowing, and where, can assist in connecting to and harmonizing with the entire group. It is the most fundamental tool in a Pagan's repertoire. By focusing on your chakras, you become aware of the flow of energy throughout your entire body and will begin to understand those flows and how they are enhanced or disrupted by outside influences. One way to do so is to use various things (stones, colors, sounds, and so on) that correspond to each chakra to focus your attention. The table on the following page provides a starting point in your attunement.

~Magickal Connections~

Chakra Correspondences

Name	Stones	Animals	Psychological	Right	Archetype
Base	Garnet, hematite, bloodstone, lodestone	Ox, bull	Survival	To have	Earth Mother
Belly	Coral, carnelian	Fish, alligator	Sexuality, emotions	To feel	Eros
Solar Plexus	Topaz, amber, citrine	Ram, lion	Power, energy	To act	Magician
Heart	Emerald, aventurine, rose quartz	Antelope, dove	Love	To love	Quan Yin
Throat	Turquoise	Dolphin, whale	Communication	To speak	Hermes
Third Eye	Lapis Lazuli	Owl, butterfly	Intuition	To see	Hermit
Crown	Amethyst	Hawk	Understanding	To know	Sage, Wisewoman

Table based on information found in *The Sevenfold Journey* by Anodea Judith and Selene Vega.

~Basic Group Dynamics~

SEEING ONE'S CHAKRAS

RELAX AND BREATHE INTO A TRANCE STATE. BRING YOUR ATTENTION TO EACH AREA OF THE BODY CORRESPONDING TO A CHAKRA, STARTING WITH THE BASE. AT FIRST, SIMPLY OBSERVE THE AREA. NOTICE ANY COLORS, FEELINGS, SENSATIONS, OR IMAGES THAT ARISE. TAKE YOUR TIME. THIS EXERCISE MAY TAKE SEVERAL SESSIONS TO COMPLETE EACH OF THE SEVEN CHAKRAS.

AS YOU GROW MORE FAMILIAR WITH EACH ONE OF THE CHAKRAS, EXTEND THIS EXERCISE INTO THE NEXT ONE.

CLEARING THE CHAKRAS

RELAX AND BREATHE INTO A TRANCE STATE. BRING YOUR ATTENTION TO THE BASE CHAKRA. LOOK AT IT AND SEE IF THERE IS ANYTHING BLOCKING IT. LOOK ALSO TO SEE IF IT IS TOO OPEN. IT IS NOT NECESSARY TO UNDERSTAND WHY THE CHAKRA IS NOT IN BALANCE TO RETURN IT TO A BALANCED STATE, BUT AN INSIGHT MAY OCCUR TO YOU AS TO THE CAUSE OF THE PROBLEM WHILE YOU ARE WORKING WITH THAT CHAKRA. REMOVE THE BLOCKAGE BY VISUALIZING YOUR HAND REACHING IN TO CLEAN IT OFF. THINK OF USING A DUST RAG TO CLEAN OFF A LIGHT BULB: WHEN IT'S CLEAN AND BALANCED, IT WILL GLOW DEEPLY WITH ITS OWN COLOR.

CLEAR AS MANY CHAKRAS AS YOU CAN. IF YOU FIND THAT YOU ARE UNABLE TO DO THEM ALL, TRY TO COMPLETE THE "LOWER" CHAKRAS, ENDING WITH THE HEART CHAKRA, AS A GROUP IN ONE SESSION, RETURNING AT ANOTHER TIME TO START WITH THE HEART CHAKRA AND COMPLETING THE "UPPER" ONES.

ANOTHER ELEMENT OF CLEARING ONE'S CHAKRA IS TO CHECK OUR "CORDS," THE CONNECTIONS WE MAKE TO EACH OTHER. IN MOST CASES, THE CORDS LOOK THIN YET STRONG AND LEAD INTO OR OUT OF OUR CHAKRAS, AND ONLY TO FAMILY MEMBERS AND OTHER INTIMATES. IN A TIGHT-KNIT MAGICKAL GROUP, THE CORDS LINK US TO ONE OTHER AND ARE A SIGN OF A MAGICKAL GROUP'S HEALTH.

AT OTHER TIMES, THE CORDS MAY BE A HINDRANCE, OR PLACED UPON US WITHOUT OUR DESIRE OR CONSENT. THESE CORDS WILL MOST LIKELY INTERFERE WITH POSITIVE ENERGY FLOWS AND SHOULD BE REMOVED. THIS REMOVAL CAN HAPPEN AT THE SAME TIME AS WHEN YOU ARE CLEANING YOUR CHAKRAS, OR IN A SESSION DESIGNED SOLELY FOR THIS PURPOSE. I FIND THE IMAGE OF "UNPLUGGING" THE CORD TO BE MORE SOOTHING THAN THAT OF CUTTING OR OTHERWISE SEVERING THE CONNECTION.

Creating a Group Mind

Witches do magick. It is a process intricately worked within our name and the fabric of our beings. To do magick within a group requires that the entire group focus upon a desired outcome. To be that intent, in part, requires that you trust that your partners will be acting in accord with the outcome.

Group magick requires that the individual psyches within the magickal group be fused into a singular entity, which is called the Group mind. In *Applied Magic*, Dion Fortune says, "[T]he Group mind is built up out of the many contributions of many individualized consciousnesses concentrating on the same idea."[2] This Group mind, once formed, has its own momentum, amplifying the power of single individuals. It is not conscious in a self-reflective sense—that is, having an awareness of its own being. The Group mind focuses and directs the combined will of the magickal group. As a result, the power and efficacy of magickal actions is multiplied exponentially. I believe magickal groups should do ritual, and frequently. "What could be more conducive," asks Fortune, "to the formation of a powerful Group mind than...an occult ritual?"[3]

The principle of the Group mind states that energy generated from the combining of like minds is geometrically greater than the sum of its parts. In other words, minds that are focused together upon a common theme create a mutual force that is not merely additive, but vastly more powerful than any one individual

~Basic Group Dynamics~

or group of individuals. The Group mind phenomenon is constantly in effect, though people rarely notice it. It is very likely that any time two or more persons are in proximity to one another, or even when they have similar thoughts but are separated by great physical distances, some Group mind effect is taking place. The consciousness we all possess is very fluid and permeable. It flows from person to person in an automatic fashion, and the self-aware individual can cause it to flow and render specific effects according to his or her will. Each of us can and does feel energy, emotion, and intent from others on a daily basis. We know when someone has a friendly or hostile vibe even without any cues given by words or physical gestures. All of us are psychically sensitive to some degree, and when this sensitivity is refined in meditation, it becomes obvious that thoughts and feelings are very often a group phenomenon, rather than just a personal experience.

The energy we share and nurture serves to bond us together, linking us within the circle. We become a group of networked individuals, the way a grove of trees in the middle of a field is. To the outsider, each tree is a separate organism, but underneath the earth our roots merge into one another and we become one organism. We support one another and grow stronger in turn from the bond. The Group mind grows stronger.

~Magickal Connections~

The Astral Temple

One of the ways to strengthen the Group mind is to participate in the creation of an astral temple. Generally, it takes a few guided visualizations within a ritual for members to get a feel for the place. The astral temple is an excellent common place to meet to work on group issues. When visualizing the astral temple, it is better to leave the description a bit open-ended, with only a few constants. Different members of the group will see alternate appearances or aspects of even the most basic items, whereas other things are seen the same way, even when they are not specifically described. The aspects will tend to change over time, with some things seen early on, and then never again, or reappearing after long absences.

Building an astral temple is not something I would do immediately upon forming the magickal group, as it requires a great deal of comfort and an already-burgeoning Group mind to accomplish successfully. Creating and using an astral temple helps to build the Group mind of a magickal group, connecting the members of the working community together and providing a sacred space that is accessible even over great distances. It is a refuge, a place of learning, and a holding place for the energies and power of the assembly.

The temple grows stronger with use. Its creation can take place in a single ritual, or with a series, mirroring the building of a physical structure (laying the foundation, erecting the pillars, marking spaces for the different rooms, and so on). In my Tradition, both Yule and Imbolc are excellent times to begin this group endeavor. The creation of the temple is a group project, and I strongly recommend that the group reach consensus about how it looks before performing the ritual.

~Basic Group Dynamics~

Describing Our Astral Temple

MEET IN CIRCLE, PERHAPS EVEN CASTING A FORMAL CIRCLE TO CHARGE THE SPACE. DESIGNATE A PERSON (OR SEVERAL, ONE AT A TIME) TO TAKE NOTES.

EACH PERSON TAKES A TURN AT DESCRIBING HOW THE TEMPLE LOOKS IN GENERAL (FOR EXAMPLE, "IT HAS GREEK COLUMNS," "THE WALLS ARE MADE OF EGYPTIAN SANDSTONE," "IT'S VERY SIMPLE WITH CLEAN LINES AND UNCLUTTERED SPACE," "I SEE A FANTASTICAL GOTHIC WIZARD'S WORKROOM," AND SO ON). MAKE A LIST OF COMMON ELEMENTS. ARE THERE SPECIFIC ELEMENTS THAT ARE ABSOLUTELY NOT APPROPRIATE/ALLOWED? (MY GROUP, FOR EXAMPLE, HAS A MEMBER WHO IS TERRIFIED OF SNAKES, SO WE HAVE MADE A POINT OF NO SNAKE IMAGERY WITHIN OUR ASTRAL TEMPLE.)

DO THE DIFFERENT DIRECTIONS/ELEMENTS HAVE ENTIRELY DIFFERENT AREAS OF THE TEMPLE? IF SO, DO THEY LOOK RADICALLY DIFFERENT FROM OTHER SECTIONS? (THE DIFFERING STYLES CAN APPEAL TO DIFFERENT MEMBERS, ALLOWING SOME PORTION OF THE TEMPLE TO APPEAL TO EVERYONE.) IS THE ALTAR CENTRAL TO THE TEMPLE? IS THE TEMPLE OPEN OR CLOSED?

~Magickal Connections~

ARE PARTICULAR MEMBERS DRAWN TO SPECIFIC AREAS? THE GROUP MAY DECIDE TO ASSIGN PAIRS TO EACH DIRECTION/ELEMENT, WITH THE LEADER RESPONSIBLE FOR THE ALTAR AREA.

FINALLY, HOW WILL YOU GET THERE? WHAT ELEMENTS WILL ALWAYS BE PRESENT, CREATING "TRIGGERS" WITHIN THE MAGICKAL MIND. FROM THESE NOTES AND DISCUSSIONS DECIDE WHAT THE TEMPLE WILL LOOK LIKE, AND FILL IN THE DETAILS OF THE ASTRAL TEMPLE RITUAL THAT FOLLOWS.

Creating an Astral Temple Ritual

Cast the circle and call the quarters, focusing on the protective aspects of each element. If your magickal group has specific deities or a pantheon it works with, call upon them to guide your group in the ritual. If not, then I recommend Athena, Cerridwen, Hermes/Mercury, Thoth, or Isis.

Relax and get comfortable, then move into trance using your favorite trance induction. Choosing one that has a journey motif is a good idea; it will provide a smoother transition into the guided meditation portion of the ritual.

When everyone is relaxed and deeply in trance, say:

"You find yourself walking along a path through a dense forest. The trees are close together and little light can be seen from above. It is very quiet, only the occasional animal sound disturbs the peace. You are looking for a place, a place you have only been told of, but you know it exists. The path sharply turns ahead, and you find yourself at the base of a large hill. Set deeply into the side of the hill is a doorway. The door is locked.

You reach into your pocket and pull out a key. Use it to unlock the door and enter the temple. This place is sacred and secure.

On the other side of an entryway is a doorway. Within the temple there are four gates, towers, pillars, or doorways at the quarters in your temple leading to other places. You will explore them later."

Describe the temple as everyone had agreed upon. (Perhaps have each person describe a specific section.) Return to the center and examine the entire area of your temple. Create the details of your surroundings. In the center, manifest your altar and circle space. When the temple is constructed as you all have agreed, gather in the center. Hold hands and chant:

As we will, so mote it be!

Bless this space. Blessed be!

Feel the love and pure energy of your group fill the temple with joyous energy. Let it consecrate the space completely. When you are ready, return to the material plane using the same path that brought you there, making sure to lock the door behind you.

Creating Perfect Love and Perfect Trust

"Perfect love and perfect trust" is a foundation element within many magickal circles, but it cannot be granted, or assumed, from the start. I know that I never immediately trust and love a person newly met, no matter how "good" her energy feels, how many past lives we've spent together, and how much she likes me. Contrast the positive vibrations of my mythical encounter with the cool impersonality of the text-based online environment, and you can see why this issue is even more difficult for cyber groups.

However, if you look at "perfect love, perfect trust" as an ideal, and see it in its proper context with intimacy, it becomes easier to understand. Intimacy is not sexual. Instead, it is the acceptance of another's nature, while at the same time being aware of your needs and able to articulate them. Intimacy is much closer to equality than sexuality. When intimacy is present in a group, you are entering a circle, sacred space, and your love and trust allow you to act in accord with the larger group to do magick and to connect with the Divine. It becomes an expression of our achieving union with our Higher Self, that part of us that acts in accord with the highest purpose of the Universe, as well as with the God/desses we love and worship. In a sense, entering the sacred circle allows one to shed all negative personal aspects, and so become "Perfect." (This does not work if you are actively in a state of discord with another member of the group, but I will talk about that later.) You cannot force intimacy; it is grown, the way a tender plant is in a desert environment. To try and "prove" perfect love and trust is to invite the dissolution of your group. Some groups create it by working skyclad, others by having a story-telling session focusing on a single theme (food, sex, death, mothers, and so on), and still others just wait for it to develop organically.

Intimacy

Intimacy comes from relationships that exist over time, from the delicate dance we engage in between separateness and connectedness with others in our lives. It is unrelated to intensity of emotion or the romantic pairing with another. Intimate relationships are those that do not operate at the expense of the self, and where our selves do not operate at the expense of others.

The self is an amalgam of traits and perspectives that we have put together from lives where we are told to "be yourself!" while at the same time subjected to signals to conform, get along, or "fit in." The survival of our relationships with our primary caregivers is based on our being a certain way or playing a specific role within the group if only because learning what others expect of us is a necessary part of being a civilized human. Our "true self" does not form within a vacuum. But a healthy self is one that is being who she is rather than what others want, expect, or need her to be while allowing others to do the same.

I recently had a student leave my class because his wife of several decades felt that his newfound beliefs were changing their marriage for the worse. (Specifically, although she realized he was not worshiping the devil, to her he was no longer aligned with God and that was intolerable.) She'd given him an ultimatum and he chose her over Wicca. This was a difficult situation for me, because as his mentor I'd heard him tell me many times how unhappy his marriage had been. But I recognized a curious dynamic taking place in this situation: His deepening knowledge of Wicca had shown him a new way of living, one that brought him joy. Although he was happier, he was also doing things without her, and making other (more subtle) changes. After 20+ years of sameness she felt threatened. My magickal group discussed this situation in a variety of settings, and finally accepted that his decision was his choice (with an undercurrent of "its a bad choice") and that, as much as we didn't like it, we understood why he would do so.

We know there is a price to pay when we betray the self, but we cannot know with much certainty the price we pay for making a change instead of betraying the self. In my student's case, the price would be the loss of his marriage, just at a time when he'd found renewed joy in it. Rarely is the cost or benefit so obviously seen. So we come to understand that to change requires courage, but the failure to change does not indicate a lack of courage. Blame is not required, only understanding and patience. If we can accept the fact that all we are and all we do now has evolved for a good reason then we can understand that it serves an important purpose.

We all need people and are deeply affected by our interactions with others, and the creation of an authentic self does not require that we shun all relationships. Instead, we can come to understand ourselves as authentic when we:

- Understand ourselves as a balanced picture of strength and weaknesses.
- Articulate our priorities, beliefs, and values, while at the same time living in accordance and support of them.
- Engage others regarding difficult and painful issues.
- Disagree with others and allow them to do the same.

In JaguarMoon we have several avenues available to us. First of all, new members come to us only after spending a year in our Art of Ritual class, so they know us, and we know them, and they generally have formed a tight bond with their mentor after working with her/him for the year. We spend time at each coven meeting taking as much time as we need to talk about what is going on in our lives. We listen. If asked, we contribute advice or support, but otherwise we give each member our full attention and respect for as long as s/he needs. We each make a conscious effort to get to know one another by working together on projects, such as writing new rituals or doing research for a class presentation. When we grow past a certain size, potential Initiates must find a Sponsor (who is not also her/his mentor), making yet another connection within the group.

Intimacy takes time to evolve. It is built on mutual information sharing, recognition of others' inner and outer selves, and mutual self-knowledge. You cannot force this process; you must allow it to happen and give it the care it requires. I believe that it takes a minimum of three months of continual exercises and participation before the sense of community and cohesion is felt. It may be longer still before true intimacy is present. (Chapter 6 discusses mentoring and intimacy in greater detail.)

~Basic Group Dynamics~

Meteor's Heart Ritual

This is a ritual to link the heart chakras of group members and encourage opening to one another on several levels.

Cleanse your self and your sacred space. Call the quarters, focusing on air's support in understanding others, fire's strength in sparking our admiration for others, water's ability to connect on an emotional level, and earth's strength in understanding our selves.

Invoke the Lord and Lady and ask Their assistance in strengthening your emotional openness, your ability to love another, from the heart. Relax and get comfortable. Close your eyes and take three deep breaths.

Listen to your heartbeat; its gentle pulse humming through your soul. Let it carry you inward, deeper, inward to your deepest heart.

Your breath is as the wind, your blood the sacred waters, your body grows, heavy.

Sinking deeper into the earth, your heartbeat carries you in....

You stand in a sacred place.

Look up at the night sky: it is brilliant with stars.

Leo roars above you, challenging the universe in His pride, flirting with the universe in His fortune.

Meteors fall down, thrown off his mane like sparks.

Breathe deeply of the clean, fresh air.

The light of Sirius shines down upon you, filling you with its power. You feel its pulse within you, growing stronger with each breath you take, increasing in intensity, until you are brimming with energy. *The energy begins to coalesce over your heart chakra, moving from all over your body. It thickens in the center of your chest, forming a star of its own. The light is steady, bright, and strong.*

The leader starts by saying aloud: "I, (<u>name 1</u>), link to you, (<u>name 2</u>), heart to heart." If you are alone, repeat for each person in the magickal group.

~Magickal Connections~

The next person then says: "I, (<u>name2</u>), link to you, (<u>name3</u>), heart to heart." Repeat for each person in the magickal group, ending with the High Priestess.

You stand in your sacred place, a shining ribbon of star's energy flowing from your heart to that of your magickal group siblings.

Say aloud: "We are all linked. Let it flow from you in you to you away from you in an endless ribbon, heart to heart in an open weave of laughter and love, honesty and trust."

Raise your hands high above your head, and the light follows our hands up into the sky, while the web of our energy remains intact. As it rises above us the distance between the lines grows smaller, so the strands begin to merge together.

Where there once was many, there are fewer…and soon only a single strand exists, a mobius loop of energy, endlessly flowing.

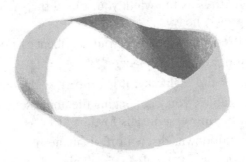

With a SHOUT release the energy, which shatters into dozens of stars, raining down as though they're meteors around us.

Say: "We are a circle, within a circle, with no beginning, and never ending. So Mote it Be!"

Thank the Deities and the elements and ground out any excess energy.

CHAPTER 6

MENTORING

Many people have an image in their minds when they think of the word *mentor*—and in many cases it is only partially accurate. Most commonly they think of an older or more experienced person who guides them to do better than they would have on their own. Spiritually speaking, a mentor is primarily concerned with establishing and clarifying spiritual growth. In practice, any person might be a mentor; the circumstances dictate who and what might be most appropriate. This chapter will discuss various aspects of acting as a mentor to others.[1]

A mentor can be a role model, a listener, a supporter, an evaluator, and a transmitter of lore. Specifically, a mentor is a:

- Sounding board.
- Guide.
- Person interested in another's development.
- Leader.
- Person willing to share his/her experience and knowledge.

~Magickal Connections~

The core responsibility is to help the seeker listen for the inner voice and change her/his life to be in increasing harmony with that inner direction. A mentor fills many roles, often several at one time, depending on the protégé's needs and the situation. Those roles include:

1. **The communicator.** The mentor encourages the exchange of information and establishes an environment of open interaction. S/he often acts as a sounding board for the protégé's concerns.

2. **The counselor.** The mentor works with the protégé to identify skills and abilities, as well as areas of personal development. Goal-oriented, this relationship revolves around strategic planning to achieve personal goals.

3. **The coach.** The mentor identifies developmental needs for improved performance and focuses on how the protégé works within a larger group. Similar to that of the counselor, the coach is more concerned with leadership and technical skills.

4. **The advisor.** The mentor recommends training opportunities from which the protégé could benefit, as well as appropriate strategies for direction. Playing a directive role, the mentor reviews the protégé's development regularly and helps him/her identify obstacles to growth as well as appropriate actions to resolve the blockage.

5. **The broker.** The mentor acts as a "go-between," facilitating the protégé's relationships with others. The "others" may be people of status, opportunities for growth, peers, or others who would benefit from the association.

For every mentor, there is a protégé, a person who wants to develop his or her potential. A protégé is, essentially, someone with the ability and desire to develop her/his skills, perhaps even as a leader. An ideal protégé will be an active participant in the mentoring relationship. S/he will:

- ◉ Proactively communicate expectations.
- ◉ Notify mentor of problems or concerns.
- ◉ Act responsibly.
- ◉ Be prepared (and prompt) for meetings.
- ◉ Be open to new ideas.
- ◉ Accept constructive criticism.
- ◉ Demonstrate initiative.
- ◉ Be aware of, and actively working on, strengths and weaknesses.

Guidelines

A mentor is primarily a role model and is therefore charged with continually developing and expanding his/her own spiritual growth. Many analogies describe Paganism as one of many paths to the Source, or the Divine. Mentoring, then, is akin to the people who help us through the wilderness as we travel. They do not know it all, but they have been on this trail before and can provide assistance as to what lies ahead. We still need to walk the path, but we are better prepared for the obstacles encountered. Judy Harrow recommends that we think of our protégés as Pagans with a new vocation applying to us as apprentices,[2] and I think this is a wise beginning.

The spiritual mentoring environment may vary by circumstance and timing, but will always require a high level of trust. The freedom to explore (go off on a tangent) is an integral part of the process, facilitated by open discussions and a low level of risk imparted by a clearly tolerant mentor. Privacy is maintained, as is a focus on developing character along with skills. The ability to provide such a safe environment comes with a relationship that stands outside of normal hierarchies. It is one where the two parties interact with one another as adults (despite true age) and not as teacher/student or master/apprentice. Although the mentoring relationship is that of an elder "bringing a newcomer along," it is outside of traditional roles. Ideally, the mentor will learn as much from a protégé (if in a different area) as s/he will impart.

Crucially, the mentor is responsible *to* the protégé, but not responsible *for* the protégé, distinctly different from that of the teacher/student relationship. The spiritual mentor is interested in developing the entire person: talent, character, mentality, and ethics.

Mentoring is a time commitment. It may be a few hours each week or more, depending on the situation and requirements. For example, at the beginning of the mentor/protégé relationship there may be a lot of time spent together as each person gets to know the other and defines the path of learning together. If there is a specific goal to attain, the timing of success may require an intense period of commitment. If the protégé has an area that requires a great deal of work, the time spent will vary according to progress made. In fact, if we do not feel a call to mentor, we probably should not.

In the mentoring process, each participant has specific obligations to fulfill:

Protégé	Mentor
Prepare specific goals.	Track progress on goals.
Review goals.	Review goals.
Discuss options.	Critique progress (constructively).
Decide on direction.	Provide options.
	Encourage autonomy of protégé.

~Mentoring~

In considering whether to accept someone as a protégé, take the time to go through an evaluation and assessment; examine your preferences and limits. For example, if I was considering a protégé, my evaluation would look this way:

Likely to accept if protégé:

◉ Was recommended by a respected other (my mentor, for example, or a peer)—in this case the source is as valuable as the protégé.

◉ Is a good friend. This has its pitfalls, of course, but if you have been friends for years and s/he is only now coming to understand that the path of Paganism is for her/him, who better to act as a guide than you?

May accept if protégé:

◉ Is someone to whom I have an obligation, maybe a relative or someone who did a good deed for which training is the payment? Or, perhaps someone I already deferred, and the reason for doing so is no longer valid.

◉ Comes at a time when I foresee having the time to mentor. Perhaps a current protégé is moving on, or life has changed to allow more time for mentoring.

Unlikely to accept if protégé:

◉ Is immature (regardless of calendar age) or unstable.

◉ Seems to have too many responsibilities already.

◉ Has conflicting priorities. This is different from having too many responsibilities in that it refers to the protégé living with conflict over his or her religious choice. His/her mate may be of a different faith, for example, and sees witchcraft as evil;

or he/she is a legal minor without parental permission to study witchcraft; or he/she has a past (negative) history with others in your tradition.

There are other considerations, of course.

The Mentor's Needs

TAKING THE TIME TO EXPLORE YOUR LIMITS AND SATISFYING YOUR NEEDS IS THE FIRST VITAL STEP IN THE MENTORING RELATIONSHIP. BEFORE TAKING ON THIS ROLE, ASK YOURSELF:

- *What are your areas of expertise?*
- *What areas are you deficient in?*
- *What are your core spiritual values?*
- *What are your preferred teaching and learning styles?*
- *Where are you within the web of your magickal group and/or Tradition? What are the next steps to achieve, and how will mentoring support (or detract from) your ability to achieve that step?*
- *What kinds of personalities/attitudes/mannerisms are offensive or difficult for you to deal with?*

It can be difficult to be a mentor, but the benefits are well worth the time and energy spent on the process. It is a learning experience (every protégé has something to teach in turn) and a way to keep the knowledge "sharp" as you discover new ways to say the same old thing. It is an old saw among teachers, no less so for being true, that you really only master a skill when you can teach it effectively. It is satisfying to know that you are not only helping another's development (a process you can literally see) but also that what you are doing benefits the greater community. Finally, you are acting as a role model for the next "generation."

~Mentoring~

Many of us worry that we aren't "good enough" to mentor another—that we haven't learned enough, or that our training is flawed. As long as we don't exaggerate our abilities or cease our own development we can offer a great deal to the person newly come to the Path.

In general, the mentor will be transmitting the community's culture to the protégé, including traditions, history, and values. As mentioned, the mentor will do this in an open atmosphere for dialogue where listening and questioning turn and turn about. Ideally, the mentor will impart specific skills and competencies from personal knowledge and growth, but may act as a facilitator and guide to how to discover that knowledge on one's own. By giving constructive feedback and evaluation, the mentor supports the protégé's progress in taking risks and increasing confidence. The mentor also acts as a tangible role model.

In my experience, mentors need to give more feedback (especially constructive criticism) and encouragement than they usually feel comfortable with. They also need to be more available and more understanding of the tensions inherent within a mentor/protégé relationship where the goal is self-development. Along with that, most mentors should avoid giving advice (although, if they must, doing it too early is problematic) and allow the protégé to spend more time figuring it out for herself/himself.

Transference is a concept borrowed from psychology and it is one of the most paradoxical processes involved in mentoring. It is essentially the unconscious redirection of feelings of one person to another, and specifically is used to describe the redirection from a significant person to the therapist or (in this case) mentor. An example of the commonality of transference in a Pagan context is the reference to a High Priestess as "Mother" and the High Priest as "Father." On the one hand transference assists the protégé in trusting the mentor. This has the benefit of encouraging the protégé to work more specifically towards his/ her goals while trusting, more deeply, the mentor's belief in the protégé's ability achieve that growth. However, it also encourages the protégé to put the mentor on a pedestal and can seduce us into wanting to be idealized. (It's a heady feeling to be seen as ideal.) Transference occurs whether we want it to or not, and it is a valuable tool. Transference is a topic larger than the scope of this book. To learn more, I recommend the works of Carl Jung.

Expectations

A good mentor will begin her relationship with a protégé by discussing each person's goals and expectations. Begin with this question: Who are we? This can start with a kind of magickal or spiritual resume or just an informal discussion. Most people I work with come to me through the class I teach, and so I have an advantage of seeing what they feel are their strengths and weaknesses early on. When we meet to form a mentoring relationship we have already established a rapport, and can concentrate on what is important to each of us. Generally, asking (and recording) what each hopes to gain from the relationship is also a good beginning point. Discussing what areas are available to the protégé, as well as the progression from the current point to the next and beyond, can be fruitful as well. Not all magickal group members want to lead a group; many want to master specific skills and then pass them on to the next in turn. Others simply enjoy the participation and work involved in being in a group instead of working solitary. Knowing what each expects from the outset can prevent many a miscommunication.

At some point in the journey (it will be different for each relationship), the mentor and protégé are wise to check in as to how successful the process has been. Is each gaining as expected? Can it be improved? It is necessary to let the relationship develop and not expect too much too soon—but beware creeping stagnation. This is when each person says that "things are fine" without ever testing or pushing the relationship to see if it is fine, or just static. Each person may have different communication styles, or ambitions, and that can produce tension, but it is not a bad thing. The fact that the mentor can provide different perspectives for the protégé is valuable in and of itself. Each should be learning from the other (although it is likely the mentor is learning less than the protégé, it should not be a one-way process) and if that is not the case, ending the process with no fault levied is called for.

The *mentoring process* resembles this:

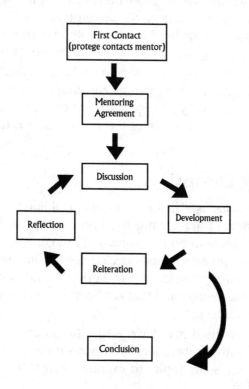

~Magickal Connections~

When we work with others to advance their spirituality, we are moving into difficult territory. We are engaging in a process of profound self-evaluation and confrontation, clearing away the dross to make way for spiritual and personal growth. Many branches of Paganism are difficult spiritual pathways when done well. Individual responsibility is a core tenet of these branches and to manifest that requires constant work. We are given powerful tools and using them properly demands compassion, wisdom, respect, and restraint—all of which requires confronting our demons on an ongoing basis. Doing so unprepared, however, can throw us into a state of crisis. Spiritual difficulty can manifest in the physical realm and closely resemble mental illness. Hopefully, this is a temporary state, but it underscores the need for the protégé to be a sane adult with a good idea of her/his identity, boundaries, and ethics before they go looking into the deeper levels of our religion.

It is not necessary for a mentor to be available 24/7 to the protégé. Just as a loving parent encourages independence in the child, the healthy protégé will learn to explore and answer questions on her own, using the mentor as a reference and guide.

Opening Discussions

As glorious as it might seem, the likelihood that you will find a perfect fit in a mentor (or a protégé!) is unlikely. Many of us are willing to do the work, and are generous and interested in the process of self-development while maintaining a stable, mature, presence in the world. We all have our personal quirks, though, and that is where the "rub" will come in. So, where to begin?

Your tradition may have a specific program of training, complete with "icebreakers" to open up the relationship. If not, here are some topics to explore, preferably early in the relationship.

~Mentoring~

Personal history. How did you each come to Paganism? What was your early religious training (pre-Paganism) like? Are there assumptions arising out of those formative experiences?

Magickal style. Formal, informal, or totally inexperienced? Shamanistic or ceremonial? Discussing the role of specific (pre-written) scripts, spontaneous declarations, and how original work works with (or against) the rituals "handed down" within a tradition is a fruitful conversation to explore.

Information dissemination/assimilation. Formal versus informal? Structured or freeform? How do you like to teach? To learn?

Expectations. What does each hope to get from the relationship? This is a good conversation to return to at regular intervals as needs change.

Techniques for Mentoring

The core technique of the mentoring relationship is that of *active listening*. This technique comes to us from psychotherapy and has three components:

- Listen with all of your attention, distractions eliminated.
- Let the speaker know you are listening by providing physical and verbal feedback.
- Remain centered throughout.

Although I first learned about active listening in college, it was an academic exercise until I worked with Samaritans of New York City. This 24-hour, all-volunteer crisis hotline relied on active listening to relieve the callers' pain. I worked with them for more than four years and will never forget the training I received.[3]

Active listening is a structured form of listening and responding that focuses the attention on the speaker. The listener attends to the speaker fully, and then repeats, in the listener's own words, what s/he thinks the speaker has said. The listener does not have to agree with the speaker—s/he must simply state what s/he thinks the speaker said. This enables the speaker to know whether the listener really understood what was said.

Listen

We live in a world of meaningless noise, and our ability to listen is usually atrophied by the time we reach adulthood. The radio plays or the TV blathers during our conversations, providing an ongoing distraction. Even when we sit in silence, we are often thinking while the other is talking, and therefore we are not listening. The act of listening can be a magickal act as we put aside ourselves to engage with the other to explore their inner self. In setting aside ourselves, we enter the other and explore; we open to the other and stay present in the moment, even in the face of intense emotions and a desire to be "objective." In doing so, we engage in an act of sacred awareness: We become aware of the sacred within the other. The technique is exquisitely simple: Listen as openly as possible, without expectation, interior response, or judgment. Don't theorize, or plan your response. Just listen.

For some, having someone *listen* to them is unusual, and may be something that has never happened to them before. It can make them uncomfortable, and hit all sorts of negative self-esteem buttons. Being free to share painful or hurtful things and be heard without judgment is how we create the safe space in which to explore the deeper levels of spirituality. For others, listening to confusion, grief, pain, or anger is uncomfortable and there is an overwhelming urge to "fix" it. Don't. Don't offer platitudes, comfort, or rush to shut them up. Your discomfort is your own—not theirs. Breathe and be present to the limit of your ability. Allow them to share and then move along.

~Mentoring~

Listening to another is a profound gift. It requires total attention as you cannot actively listen to someone if you are doing something else (including thinking) at the same time. If you are not willing to put aside everything, including your own worries and preoccupations, then you are not truly listening.

People's speech patterns often change when they realize that you are truly listening to them. and they may stop speaking entirely. It is astonishing how little our words are paid attention to, even by our loved ones. To have someone's total attention is exhilarating and perhaps more than a little frightening. Our words suddenly have great meaning, and we become more careful in the choice, or maybe we get over-excited and start rushing through them (before the attention runs out).

By giving another your complete attention you provide concrete evidence of their value. Many of us suffer from low self-esteem and to have another person show us so literally that we are valued is a disconcerting and healing experience. It may be that we are tongue-tied in the beginning, but as repeated indications of other's esteem are made, we grow more comfortable with the attention. We grow comfortable with being valued, and so our value becomes clearer to others; we lose our ordinary self and become extraordinary.

What we value creates value; the reciprocity of esteem is a spiral outward growing larger with each interaction. Actively listening, giving total concentration to another is an expression of love. We give up our own desires, prejudices, references, and inner voices to experience the other's perspective as fully as possible. In doing so, we totally accept the other *for themselves*. This deep level of acceptance is the gift of active listening, and it allows the speaker to open up different (and more vulnerable) parts of his or her self. In doing so, the speaker and listener come to appreciate one another more deeply.

This kind of listening requires a great deal of energy; it cannot be done while driving or cooking or while preparing for sleep. It is easily interrupted and hard to find the time to engage in when we are in a hurry. We must make the time to listen to the other.

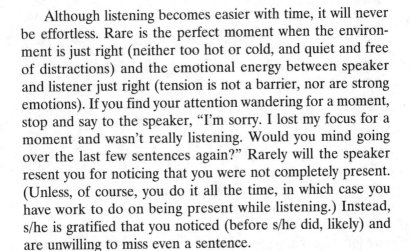

Attention Esteem Exercise

ASK A LOVED ONE (A CHILD OR A PARTNER, FOR EXAMPLE) ABOUT HIS OR HER DAY, AND GIVE THE ANSWER YOUR TOTAL ATTENTION. ASK CLARIFYING QUESTIONS AND DO YOUR UTMOST TO TURN OFF YOUR INTERNAL VOICE WHILE LISTENING (IT GETS EASIER WITH PRACTICE, I PROMISE). DO THIS EVERY DAY FOR A WEEK AND SEE WHAT COMES OF IT.

Although listening becomes easier with time, it will never be effortless. Rare is the perfect moment when the environment is just right (neither too hot or cold, and quiet and free of distractions) and the emotional energy between speaker and listener just right (tension is not a barrier, nor are strong emotions). If you find your attention wandering for a moment, stop and say to the speaker, "I'm sorry. I lost my focus for a moment and wasn't really listening. Would you mind going over the last few sentences again?" Rarely will the speaker resent you for noticing that you were not completely present. (Unless, of course, you do it all the time, in which case you have work to do on being present while listening.) Instead, s/he is gratified that you noticed (before s/he did, likely) and are unwilling to miss even a sentence.

Let Them Know You Are Listening

The act of listening to another can be profoundly transformative because it happens so rarely in our lives, but it is not enough. We must also *show* that we have been listening, proving that the space is safe. We do that by responding with acceptance and encouragement—in psychotherapy this is usually called *mirroring*. There are several ways to prove we have been listening:

- Question to clarify. *"Would you like to talk more about _____?" "Can you give me a specific example of _____?" "I would like to know more about <u>a specific aspect</u>."*

- Summarize or rephrase. *"What I understand you told me is_____."*

- Reflect feelings and beliefs. *"I hear you telling me that you feel this way about that situation."*

- Offer a tentative interpretation about the other's feelings or meaning. *"It sounds as if that really hurt you."*

- Validate. *"I bet that hurt a lot." "That must have hurt."*

- Summarize. *"You have told me the story of _____. Is that right?"*

Mirroring Exercises

SPEND A DAY, OR PORTION OF A DAY, CONSCIOUSLY MIRRORING DURING MUNDANE CONVERSATIONS. ALTER YOUR BODY LANGUAGE IN IMITATION OF THE OTHER'S POSTURE OR STANCE. JOURNAL WHAT YOU SAW AND NOTICED DURING THESE ENCOUNTERS.

ON A DIFFERENT DAY, AND IN APPROPRIATE CONTEXTS, PRACTICE VERBAL MIRRORING. THIS IS USUALLY BEST PRACTICED WITH INTIMATES—FRIENDS, LOVERS, EVEN CHILDREN—BECAUSE IT CAN BE DISCONCERTING IN THE WORKPLACE. JOURNAL WHAT YOU SAW AND NOTICED DURING THESE ENCOUNTERS.

This technique, as almost any can, can be learned, practiced, and mastered. Our society places a lot of weight on being able to speak. Think about who influences you: are they good talkers or good listeners? As we come to understand ourselves and our relationships with others, we begin to understand that communication is not limited to speaking. It is a process of truly understanding.

Remain Centered

Remaining centered is specific to the spiritual relationship (although it would be equally valid for a therapist to engage in), and to the process of creating safe space. As the mentor actively hears stories of stress, anger, and pain s/he opens herself/himself to those negative energies. By remaining centered s/he can then release that negativity and keep the self clear.

Positive Communication

THE BASIC BUILDING BLOCK OF GOOD COMMUNICATIONS IS THE FEELING THAT EVERY HUMAN BEING IS UNIQUE AND OF VALUE.

—UNKNOWN

Christine Baldwin, author of *Calling the Circle*, describes a circle as a place where people experience successful problem-solving, give and receive nurturing and appreciation, or are themselves appreciated from the heart. Further, she describes the circle as a place in which issues of difference arise and are worked out, supported by conscious awareness and encouragement by all.[4] A strong magickal group is one in which this type of dynamic and loving interaction takes place, particularly when difficult issues arise.

Every group has a flow of communication, and magickal groups are not immune to problems that are the direct result of miscommunication, misinterpretation, anger, strong-willed personalities, and power trips. (In fact, the most mediocre magickal groups can produce plots that are better than a television soap opera's.)

The truth is that humans are basically social creatures, and we like being with people. Unfortunately, our expressions are not perfect, and we frequently say one thing and mean another, or hear something and think we understand only to find out later that we were completely wrong. Some of us have nurtured the intuitive side to such a degree that we "read" body language to inform the knowledge we gain from other methods. In the physical world, using multiple forms of communication increases our ability to get our message across, as well as to understand the point being made.

Part of the weave of being a Pagan is that we accept responsibility for our own actions, including our communication. When we speak with courtesy and respect, we act out of honesty and trust. Our connection to one another is enhanced, and the group prospers. We have the responsibility to communicate our frustration with another member.

It is easy to eliminate everyone but those who agree with us in everything in our private lives. But is this why we are here? Learning from each other, especially those who differ in their worldview or background, is more difficult, but potentially more rewarding. If we truly believe we have nothing to learn from those who have different opinions on some issues, we can be certain that most of our opinions are false. I believe that it is those people with whom we have initial difficulties in understanding or appreciating that we can learn the most from.

A valuable resource for creating mutual agreements and understanding within the group is the Compact. This document can act as a safety net, defining how the group will agree to behave, and an agreement about self-governing and personal responsibility. JaguarMoon's Compact begins with a statement of purpose, briefly describes the Tradition, and then lists the five operating rules we all agree to: respect, honesty, confidentiality, accepting responsibility, and ritual attendance. It closes by noting that it will be reviewed annually so that it may reflect the changing needs of the group. Our Art of Ritual

~Magickal Connections~

Class Agreement lists 12 things expected of members, ending with their promise to take care of their family and selves before class matters. By agreeing to the same "ground rules," members are more likely to start from the same point of view and are given the same tools with which to communicate with one another. One of the more important documents I share with the class as we begin each year is a document that outlines a series of commitments that I make to them about my behavior. I believe that because my role is that of the leader, I have special responsibilities to fulfill. (These documents can be found in the Appendices B,C, and D.)

Stating expectations at the beginning will help maintain structure when the group is going through "growing pains." But even the best of us find ourselves in situations that escalate issues rather than cool them down. In my first year, I had a student who was very smart and had a great deal of intuitive knowledge. She found the early lessons boring and expressed her low opinion to the class at large. I am sorry to say that my first response to her was a public, terse, reminder that I designed the plan to be a certain way and if she did not like it, she could leave. I was very defensive, and it was not a good example to set. My second response to her came later that day, and started off with an apology to her, in public. I then took our discussion to the more appropriate forum of private e-mail. (She stayed with the class and wound up being one of my most challenging, and rewarding, students.)

There are five specific guidelines to smoother and cooler communication (see Appendix F):

1. **Make "I" statements versus "you" statements.** Speaking for yourself and about how you feel is always better than telling someone else what you think of him or her. When you do that you attack him/her and he/she, naturally, goes on the defensive. Talking to someone through a wall is much harder

than face to face. For example: "I hate it when you barge right into discussions and take over. It makes me feel like what I am saying is unimportant" feels much different than "You are so rude! You come rushing in here and take over like nothing else is going on!" Saying "I feel..." gives information and lets other people take responsibility for their actions while you take responsibility for your own feeling.

2. **Avoid absolutes.** Couching your statements in extremes just makes what you say sound absurd and dismissible. Notice the difference between "You always barge in and never let me talk!" and "I feel like you interrupt me a lot and take over the conversation." The first statement is giving a reason to eliminate the person from your life. The second is an invitation to solve a problem.

3. **Think before you speak.** Review what you are about to say. If you were hearing it, would you be offended? Perhaps this is a message best shared privately and not in public. If you are angry at all then don't say anything. Wait a day. Talk it over with a loved one, your mentor, or another group member. Check your signals: you may have misinterpreted or misread something. If you are still angry, maybe you want to make some changes. It might be a good idea to wait another day

Always wait to speak if you are offended and hurt. Ask yourself: "What do I want to accomplish? What am I likely to accomplish?" If your first draft of an angry response says exactly what you want to say, you are probably still too angry. There is nothing to lose by waiting. It is almost never necessary to have a public disagreement. You are responsible for your communication. Being right is no excuse for being hurtful.

4. **Remember the human.** Do unto others as you would have others do unto you. Stand up for yourself, but try not to hurt people's feelings.

5. One last rule from "The Notebooks of Lazarus Long" by Robert Heinlein: **"Never argue with an idiot. Other people may not be able to tell the difference."** If you argue in public you will not enhance the group's respect for you, and you will probably make a fool of yourself. Anger is a bad way to teach someone a lesson.

As the man also said, **"Never try to have the last word. You might get it."**

CHAPTER 7

MAGICKAL GROUP LIFE-CYCLE

We cannot all sit on the same side of the Fire. A Council Fire forms a circle, not a line or a square. When we move to the side we still sit at the Fire with our Brothers and Sisters, but as we move away from one we move toward another. The circle, like the Dream Hoop, brings us ever back to where we start.

—*Luther Standing Bear, Oglala*

In Chapter 1 I discussed group structures and functions, but a more important aspect is that of group dynamics—how well does the group function, as a group, rather than just a collection of individuals. Though I am sure there are some people in the world for which the tangled intricacy of groups is as clear as a summer morning, I am not one of them. It's taken me more than two decades' of participating in a variety of Pagan-oriented situations, learning through trial and error.

A magickal group is subject to all the dynamics that arise when people from different backgrounds, holding different points of view, try to get together. These dynamics are easy to see in a group where negative politics are occurring, but they are happening all the time in a somewhat cyclical fashion. It is part of the natural process of a group to move from being warm and fuzzy, where everyone is portraying their "best" selves, through chaos and confrontation as we begin to "be real," and then into a sense of true community. The group will go through this evolutionary process from the time of its formation, dipping in and out, backward and forward into various stages. What follows here is a brief look at each stage as well as suggested ideas for coping with the issues raised by members.

Stage 1: Gathering

Traditional psychology calls the initial stage of a group *forming*. Here, personal relations are primarily characterized by dependence in that members tend to rely on safe, patterned behavior and look to the group leader for guidance and direction. Scott Peck calls this stage *pseudocommunity* and says, "…members attempt to be an instant community by being extremely pleasant to one another and avoiding all disagreement… The essential dynamic of pseudocommunity is conflict avoidance… The basic pretense is the denial of individual differences."[1] Members are on their best behavior with one another. It feels warm and fuzzy because members are acting to make each other like us, and to get comfortable with the group as a whole. I agree with Starhawk, who identifies this stage with the element of air. The group is inspired and energized. Newcomers say things such as "I've come home" and "everyone here is the same as me." Everything is fresh and new, and we feel a great freedom in that we can be whomever we want to this new community. It is the dawning time.

~Magickal Group Life-Cycle~

The task of the leader is to remember that this excitement is pleasurable but fleeting; group members desire a safe group. They want to keep things simple and to avoid controversy, so it is generally a good idea to leave overly serious topics (politics, for example) for later. Focus on orientation. Reminding the group of the purpose in being here, accessing new technologies (if appropriate), and transmitting modes of "how things are done" dominate the first stage of virtual formation. Leaders will want to encourage quiet members to participate more as well as gently dissuade the more visible members from taking all of the groups' attention. The tone and attitude the leader models here will guide future behaviors and patterns of response.

Group members will often ask themselves: *Will I be accepted or rejected? What risks will I take here? How am I similar to other people here? Different? Will I feel pressured and pushed to perform in some way? How important will I be? At the same time they may be feeling concerns and fears: I'm afraid I'll look stupid. Will I tell too much about myself? Will others like me? What if they find out what I'm really like? What if everyone rejects me? What if the group attacks me? Will I embarrass myself? What if I'm asked to do something I don't want to do? What if others can tell I'm afraid and nervous? What if I find out things about myself that I can't cope with?*

~Magickal Connections~

In this initial stage you will see:

- ◉ Silence and awkwardness.
- ◉ Impatience to "get the ball rolling."
- ◉ Confusion about what everybody is supposed to be doing.
- ◉ Gentle testing of each other, particularly the leaders.
- ◉ Requests for greater leader involvement.
- ◉ "Cocktail conversations"—safe levels of conversation.
- ◉ A vying for informal leadership, depending on the group's structure—this is rare in a hierarchical structure.

In JaguarMoon's Art of Ritual class, the month of July is spent working with the energy of gathering. We focus on making connections, getting to know one another, and helping newcomers to technology get comfortable with working and interacting online. Lessons actively begin in August and the energy of gathering continues to build. We start doing ritual with one another, and the connections become even stronger.

Throughout this stage, rituals to welcome the inspiration of Mercury or Arianrhod are especially appropriate and helpful for managing the expectations of the magickal group. Both of these deities are affiliated with inspiration, the element of air, and communication. They can bring wisdom to the leader, and assist in the flow of information between group members.

Icebreakers

THESE "GET TO KNOW YOU" GAMES CAN OPEN YOUR GROUPS UP WITH LAUGHTER.

GIVE EVERYONE A LIST OF QUESTIONS TO ASK EACH OTHER (SUCH AS NAME, PETS, HOBBIES, ASTROLOGY SIGN, OR FAVORITE FOODS). PAIR EVERYONE INTO S'S AND Q'S. S'S ARE COMPLETELY SILENT WHILE Q'S

~Magickal Group Life-Cycle~

ASK THE QUESTIONS FROM THE LIST, AND THEN PREDICT WHAT THE ANSWERS WILL BE, WRITING THE PREDICTIONS DOWN. AFTER A SET TIME LIMIT, HAVE THEM SWITCH ROLES. GATHER EVERYONE TOGETHER AGAIN AND HAVE THE PAIRS INTRODUCE ONE ANOTHER WITH THEIR PREDICTIONS, CORRECTED BY THEIR PARTNER.

ASK EVERYONE: "WHAT MADE YOU SMILE TODAY?" ENCOURAGE EVERYONE TO SHARE AT LEAST ONE THING.

PAIR EVERYONE UP AND HAVE THEM STAY IN A PAIR UNTIL THEY FIND THREE UNOBVIOUS THINGS THEY HAVE IN COMMON (HAIR COLOR DOESN'T COUNT, BUT DISCOVERING THAT THEIR GRANDMOTHERS BOTH ATTENDED WOODSTOCK DOES). WHEN THEY'VE FOUND THE HIDDEN SIMILARITIES, HAVE THEM SWITCH TO A NEW PARTNER. CONTINUE UNTIL EVERYONE HAS MADE A CONNECTION WITH AT LEAST THREE OTHERS.

Stage 2: Clearing

It has to happen eventually. After the best behavior has worn off, the group moves into a stage traditional psychology calls *storming*, or chaos. Conflict arises as members realize that they do not all share the same viewpoint. Differences become more obvious and may become more important than anything else the group does. After the false similarities of the gathering stage members may feel 'betrayed' when another person seems to change her/his mind. This feeling is especially true in members who have self-esteem issues or difficult family lives.

~Magickal Connections~

There may be wide swings in members' behavior in this stage. Because of the discomfort generated, some members may remain completely silent, whereas others attempt to dominate all conversations. Elementally, this stage corresponds with fire. Our wills are strong here and we begin to stand up for ourselves. Things are getting a little hot in the group as we begin to feel the need to be "right" and convince others they are wrong.

A leader's task is to allow this stage to unfold, as difficult as that is when you may feel as if your authority is being challenged. Reminding the group of the rules of tolerance and respect may keep things from getting too chaotic, or at least from causing harm. You may feel the need to create more and more rules in order to impose some kind of structure on something that is, essentially, uncontrollable. Resist this feeling. As well, members may encounter cultural differences that make dialogues difficult. The leader can minimize this, or at least set a good example by:

- Recognizing differences as distinct without good/bad judgments attached.
- Showing respect for everyone.
- Being flexible and ready to adapt and adjust his/her behavior, without seeming insincere.
- Being tolerant by remembering that one person's norm may not be the same as another's.
- Doing away with ethnocentrism (the tendency to judge all other groups according to your own group's standards, behaviors, and customs).

Members can assist in this process by beginning the process of bending and molding their feelings, ideas, attitudes, and beliefs to suit the group's organization. They must move from a

~Magickal Group Life-Cycle~

"testing and proving" mentality to one focused on problem-solving. At this stage, the most important trait in helping groups to move on to the next stage seems to be the ability to listen.

Working with many of the fire God/desses can assist the group throughout this stage, especially when asking for wisdom to understand the deeper needs of the group. I like to work with Pele—She who dances the destructive lava up from the earth's core and in doing so creates new islands. Any Deity who deals with creating paths—Horus comes to mind—is also good to work with for guidance through this time.

Active Listening

This exercise assists in the clearing stage as it allows people to feel a connection to one another that can transcend the fire. Arbitrarily sitting down for this type of conversation will feel awkward at first, but practice will bring comfort.

Divide the group into subgroups of three, each of who will choose the role of Speaker, Listener, or Observer. (Depending on the number of participants, you might join one of the subgroups, or just wander around listening in.) The Speaker talks about something important for no more than five minutes: job, family, a decision, a question, and so forth. (The exercise is better if the topic is something the Speaker really cares about.) The Listener practices active listening (eye contact, body language, silences, and verbal minimal encouragers), concentrating on following the Speaker's train of thought. The Observer pays attention to the Listener's verbal and non-verbal skills. Observe and count only as many behaviors (eye contact, body posture, verbal minimal encouragers, topic jumps) as you can manage and still be relatively accurate.

When the Speaker is finished, the Listener discusses the experience with the two other members of the subgroup. (What was comfortable? Difficult? Did you stay with the speaker?)

THEN THE SPEAKER WILL SHARE HIS OR HER FEELINGS ABOUT THE LISTENER'S LISTENING. (DID YOU FEEL LISTENED TO? WAS IT HELPFUL? DID THE LISTENER HAVE ANY HABITS YOU FOUND DISTRACTING?) THE OBSERVER WILL THEN SHARE OBSERVATIONS. THIS SHARING PROCESS SHOULD TAKE ABOUT THREE OR FOUR MINUTES.

EVERYONE CHANGE PLACES. HAVE THE LISTENER BECOME THE SPEAKER; THE SPEAKER, THE OBSERVER; AND THE OBSERVER, THE LISTENER. GO THROUGH THE FIVE MINUTES OF TALKING AND LISTENING AND FIVE MINUTES OF EXCHANGING REMARKS TWICE MORE SO THAT EACH PERSON TAKES EACH ROLE ONCE. THE ENTIRE PRACTICE SESSION SHOULD TAKE ABOUT 25 MINUTES.

WHEN EVERYONE HAS TAKEN A TURN AT THE THREE ROLES, RE-FORM THE LARGER GROUP AND SHARE YOUR EXPERIENCES. HOW ARE THESE SKILLS RELEVANT TO YOUR WORK? WHERE ELSE WOULD THEY BE USEFUL? GO AROUND THE GROUP SO THAT PARTICIPANTS HAVE A CHANCE TO SHARE AT LEAST ONE THING THEY HAVE LEARNED ABOUT THEMSELVES IN THIS EXERCISE.

Stage 3: Building

Having been through the fire, moving to the building stage comes almost as a relief, but in some ways this can be the most challenging part of the cycle. Ideally, group members are engaged in active acknowledgment of all contributions, and there is an active sense of community-building and ongoing problem-solving. The group has learned that disagreement does not mean rejection, and deep feelings of trust begin to form. It is during this stage of development (assuming the group gets this far) that people begin to experience a sense of true community.

Water is the element that corresponds with the building stage. Much of what we deal within in this stage is the truth that lies beneath our surface Selves. Unconscious patterns of behavior and needs become more visible. We move into the realm of real emotions, and a feeling of intimacy forms within the group. Resembling water pouring from a jar, we are emptying ourselves of preconceptions. In this stage we are washing away prior (negative) training and allowing ourselves to experience one another emotionally, as full humans, rather than sharing only those parts of ourselves we deem acceptable.

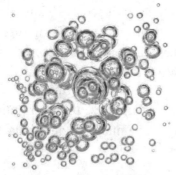

Guiding the group through this stage may sound easier, but that is an impression that dissolves when we look below the surface. Although we have begun to understand the potential for true community, we are not yet experiencing it (at least, not all the time, although we may be granted glimpses.) There are many negative patterns and past trained behaviors that will rise now, obstacles that hinder members' ability to experience the groups' dynamics. There can be a sense of fear that expressing true feelings will result in disaster—either because it provokes argument within the group (and a slide back into clearing), or because the response is not what the speaker hoped for. It is likely that the group will frequently "backslide" and re-enter the chaos of clearing.

In this stage, it is the leader's task to understand that sometimes it is necessary to take a step back and clarify needs and expectations before the group can continue forward again. (Not only is it is probably necessary, it is healthy.) The leader should be asking:

- ◉ Are individuals empowered?
- ◉ Are they more important than the group?

~Magickal Connections~

- Are tension and conflict viewed as natural elements in the problem-solving process?
- Are openness, directness, probing, and emotions not only acceptable, but necessary?
- What is the level of secrecy within the group?
- Is independent, critical thinking supported?
- Do we have unconditional respect and personal regard for each other?
- Is the process more important than the results?
- Does there always have to be a solution?
- Do members maintain a healthy balance between life in and life outside the group?

All members can assist in moving through this stage by doing their own work of uncovering their deeper selves, looking to find authenticity and truth. They can work to understand their Selves, as well as others, and provide safe space and comfort when unable to engage other members. Almost inevitably, trust issues will arise. Treating their emergence with compassion and an open heart can ease the pain for the emerging Self. Members can change preconceived ideas or opinions based on facts presented by other members, and actively ask questions of one another. A healthy sign is that members seek to share leadership—not for power, but for shared responsibility.

Water Deities are wonderful guides throughout this stage. The mythological cycle of Isis and Osiris may provide you with particularly useful insights as to moving forward and then back before moving forward again through a period of transformation.

~Magickal Group Life-Cycle~

THESE EXERCISES ENCOURAGE GROUP MEMBERS TO BUILD TRUST IN ONE ANOTHER, DEEPENING THEIR CONNECTIONS.

Taffy Pull

DIVIDE THE GROUP INTO TWO TEAMS: TAFFY AND PULLERS. HAVE EVERYONE REMOVE ANY SHARP JEWELRY OR OTHER ADORNMENT. THE TAFFY PEOPLE SIT DOWN AND LINK ARMS, LEGS, AND BODIES INTO A TANGLED MESS. THE PULLERS TRY TO GENTLY PULL THE TAFFY APART INTO HUMAN-SIZED BITS. REMIND THE PULLERS THAT THE BEST TAFFY IS MADE BY USING SMOOTH STRETCHES; IF YOU PULL TOO HARD THE TAFFY WILL SNAP. TAFFY CAN DECIDE FOR ITSELF HOW MUCH S/HE WANTS TO REMAIN A PART OF THE TAFFY MASS.

Trust Circle

EVERYONE STANDS IN A TIGHT CIRCLE, SHOULDER TO SHOULDER, FACING IN. ONE PERSON STANDS IN THE CENTER OF THE CIRCLE, WITH FEET TOGETHER AND ARMS AT HIS/HER SIDES. WHEN S/HE IS READY, S/HE CLOSES HIS/HER EYES AND GENTLY FALLS TO ONE SIDE OF THE CIRCLE. GROUP MEMBERS FACING THE CENTRAL PERSON GENTLY CATCH HIM/HER AND PASS HIM/HER ACROSS AND AROUND THE CIRCLE. (FEET REMAIN IN THE CENTER.) THE GOAL IS TO GENTLY PASS THE PERSON, NOT THROW HIM/HER BACK AND FORTH ACROSS A HUGE CIRCLE. BE GENTLE IF SOME MEMBERS ARE UNABLE TO "LET GO." HONOR THEIR STRENGTH AND ABILITY TO CARE FOR THEMSELVES IN STATING THEIR NEEDS.

Trust Walk

HAVE THE GROUP LINE UP HOLDING HANDS. DESIGNATE ONE OF THE PEOPLE AT THE END OF THE LINE THE LEADER. EVERYONE ELSE CLOSES THEIR EYES (OR IS BLINDFOLDED) AND THE LEADER LEADS THEM OVER, UNDER, AROUND, AND THROUGH VARIOUS OBSTACLES. THE LEADER MUST GUIDE THE PERSON DIRECTLY BEHIND HER/HIM BY VOCAL AND/OR TACTILE DIRECTIONS, AND THAT PERSON MUST DO THE SAME TO THE "BLIND" PERSON BEHIND HER/HIM, AND ON DOWN THE LINE. THIS EXERCISE CAN ALSO BE DONE IN PAIRS.[2]

The first three stages are ones that every group will go through repeatedly—many groups never make it past the gathering stage (particularly online), and a large number will go from gathering into clearing and then back to gathering several times over before moving on to building. It is also common for a group to drop from building into clearing on regular occasions—particularly if it's a task-oriented magickal group. Accomplishing a task can drop the group back into clearing or gathering until it redefines its new goal.

The next stage is much more rarely attained.

Stage 4: Community

With community we see individual members are self-assured and confident; the need for group approval is past. The group is both highly task- and people-oriented. There is unity: Group identity is clear, group morale is high, and group loyalty is intense. Differences are neither hidden nor highlighted, but are accepted and valued. This stage corresponds with earth. It is difficult to achieve this stage, and, having attained it, not every group will retain it. It is common for the group to return to an earlier stage and move onward from there. If group members are able to evolve to this stage, there is an expansion to true interdependence.

~Magickal Group Life-Cycle~

The feeling here is: We have explored together, fought with one another, earned respect, and made a place with one another that we call community. Now we can move deeper into our knowledge, having found that place, that home.

To bring your group to this stage is an accomplishment about which all members should feel very proud. The most common manifestation of this step is that the individual members begin to ask themselves, "What part of me must die so that my true Self can be born?" And they will answer by making large changes within their lives. A woman in an emotionally dead long-term relationship will start seeing a counselor. A man who allowed his wife to gain full custody of their children begins to explore the possibility of sharing responsibility with her once again. Someone who never saw herself as a writer begins to create the book you now hold.

The biggest pitfall here is that the group may begin to believe that this stage is the end of the cycle. That you have taken your group the end, as if the journey is completed and there are no further destinations. This stage is not a goal, such as winning a race, or completing a project; it is a way-station along the journey. You may slide back into other stages as group members come and go, or as the group evolves a different focus and intent from the original. It may be a planned re-cycling to re-energize and re-connect with the energy of gathering, for example.

The earth-ruling Deities will guide you here, and I recommend Demeter and Cernunnos in particular. Expanding your circle to include the surrounding community and thinking of continuity are areas all members are encouraged to consider throughout this stage.

Stage 5: Release

Release is the final stage in many senses. It is the most difficult and one where the pain may be greatest for all members.
Although, technically, all groups go through this stage, many
do not do so formally or with intent. Therefore, for me, not all
groups arrive at this stage, which involves the formal closing of
the group and the ending of current relationships. Many groups
will end (generally while moving through stages two or three),
but a planned end may well be called for in time. The most
effective interventions in this stage are those that facilitate task
termination and the disengagement process.

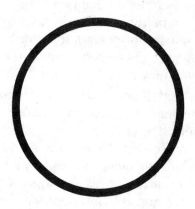

Spirit is the guiding element here, the energy that assists
us as we move from the physical plane to that of the immate-
rial. Our bonds, once so strong and supportive, become memories and lessons learned. A planned end usually includes
recognition for participation and achievement and an opportunity for members to say personal goodbyes. Concluding a
group can create some apprehension—in effect, a minor crisis. The termination of the group is a regressive movement
from giving up control to giving up inclusion in the group.

~Magickal Group Life-Cycle~

There is no single Deity to ask for guidance throughout this period, so prayers to the One, the All, or the Source may be especially useful.

Ritual to Release or Close a Group

Preparation:

- ◉ Re-arrange the group or your personal altar. Clean it, and spend time with the sacred objects.
- ◉ Choose a memory of a special moment within the group.

Items needed/ritual setup:

- ◉ Incense (sandalwood is especially appropriate).
- ◉ Oil for self-blessing (or water with salt, or water with herbs).
- ◉ A long piece of cord, rope or other fairly thick piece of string.

Cast the Circle.

Call the Quarters.

Invoke the God/dess.

The ritual leader opens with,

"My friends, now is the time to recognize our own Divinity. Let us bless our Self....

I bless my feet that they walk the path You lay before me.

I bless my knees that they may kneel at Your altar.

I bless my sex that all acts of love and pleasure be Yours.

I bless my womb (belly), heart of my creative fire.

I bless my breasts (chest) formed in strength and beauty.

I bless my shoulders that I may lightly carry the burdens of life.

I bless my hands that I may do Your work.

~Magickal Connections~

I bless my lips that I may sing Your praises.

I bless my "Eye" (Third eye) that I may See what you show me.

I bless my Self that I may recognize You within me.

So mote it be!"

The ritual leader holds up a long piece of cord.

"My friends, you see before you the cord of the (<u>name of group</u>)." The ritual leader ties a half-slip knot loosely in the cord. "My friends, this knot is our connection with one another through this time." The ritual leader shares his/her memory, and finishes with "All dreams come true."

The ritual leader turns to his/her right and rolls the knot along the cord to that person. The second person shares his/her memory, and finishes with "All dreams come true." (The knot is pushed along the cord, all around the circle as each person shaves their memory. The last person pushes it back to the ritual leader after saying "All dreams come true.")

The ritual leader takes the knot and then rolls it off the cord's end, where it disappears.

"My friends, as this knot has gone, so too has our connection to (<u>name of group</u>). Blessed be!"

Bid farewell to the God/dess.

Bid farewell to the Quarters and open the Circle.

Potential Problems

> I'LL TELL YOU ALL MY SECRETS/ BUT I LIE ABOUT MY PAST.
> —TOM WAITS ("TANGO TILL THEY'RE SORE")

For much of this book I have discussed the work of participating in a magickal group, the responsibility inherent in leading it, and some of the fun aspects of switching roles. I would be doing you a disservice if I were to ignore the uncomfortable things that arise in groups.

~Magickal Group Life-Cycle~

If you thought that creating or participating in a magickal group would free you from backbiting politics, unfulfilled expectations, or lack of cohesiveness that plagues any mundane group, you were wrong. Hopefully, my experiences will give you some idea of what to expect, what to do if the situation arises, and how to avoid the worst situations.

A magickal group is subject to all the dynamics that arise when people from different backgrounds, holding different points of view, come together. It is part of the natural process of a group to move from being warm and fuzzy, where everyone is portraying their "best" selves, through chaos and confrontation as we begin to "be real," and finally into a sense of true community.

Other than the evolutionary issues, there are three categories where problems are likely to arise: cohesiveness, conflict, and continuity. The next three chapters will discuss these problems in detail.

CHAPTER 8

MAINTAINING COHESIVENESS

To endure is greater than to dare; to tire out hostile fortune; to be daunted by no difficulty; to keep heart when all have lost it—who can say this is not greatness?

—*William Makepeace Thackeray*

Cohesion is the sense of belonging, of participation. Some groups quickly achieve a cohesive identity; others struggle to find it or ultimately disband. Although creating a sense of cohesion is always a problem for both physical and cyber magickal groups, I believe it is more difficult to achieve online.

As I discussed in Chapter 5, intimacy takes time to evolve. It is built on mutual information sharing, recognition of the other's inner as well as outer self, and mutual self-knowledge. Some members may participate in the process of creating intimacy, of sharing information, and yet never feel as if they are members of the same group. I have had people tell me they were leaving after spending a year or more with me and, when I asked why, they said that they felt they were outsiders. They never felt that they had formed deep bonds with the rest of the coven. It was a valuable lesson for me that we could experience the same event and yet perceive it very differently.

Negative Self-Images

One of the more subtle mechanisms for preventing intimacy, and thus cohesion, within the group is participants' negative self-image. It is a common trait in the everyday world, but nothing compares to listening to someone talk (or read their words) to clearly see how they see themselves. When somone says "I know this is a stupid question..." or "I know this is dumb, but..." they are expressing a feeling of low self-worth. She is expressing her feelings, which is great, because it is very likely that there is another member who is thinking those words and yet cannot express them to the larger group. The silent self-haters are the ones who generally will end up drifting away or will leave after a time, not always telling you why, but going nonetheless.

Humans are relentless self-criticizers, and that interferes with our self-respect. Whether we heard negative criticism as children, or created it in response to cultural feedback, we repeat it endlessly and suffer from its effects. In the circle, our inner loop of self-criticism interferes with our ability to connect with one another. "She is so beautiful. Why would she want to be with a person like me?" "Her life is so smooth and perfect; she won't understand my difficulties." These kinds of thoughts drown out the truth: that everyone else is sharing pieces of our experience, and we can understand one another's flaws far more easily than our perfection.

If you are a leader, you will be held up to an interesting mirror. You will be aware of your imperfections and, if you have done the work, you are comfortable with those flaws. (If not exactly comfortable, then understanding and eventually forgiving.) Those around you may be unwilling to accept the imperfections, however, and will want to place you on that metaphorical pedestal, one step down from the Divine. At the same time, if you seem too perfect, those around you will begin to feel that you can't understand them, and they may stop telling you their problems. Perhaps they will feel you will think less of them, or that they are unworthy. What an unhealthy dynamic!

In my first coven, I worked with a lovely woman, a powerful witch who seemed very strong and capable, always speaking her truth. As we worked together I began to realize that she was having difficulties with another group in which she and her husband were also members. That group practiced a tradition in which sex was a part of every ritual[1] and the leader maintained control over members through a combination of sexual dominance, mental manipulation, and other tactics designed to eliminate members' self esteem. When she told us of these practices, we offered her love and support while encouraging her to get out of there. Instead, she chose to view our actions as interfering, and became disruptive when the group met. As much as we hated to do so, we had to ask her to leave. Her pain and self-hatred turned against us, and it was too destructive to the coven. What I learned was this: Some people can never let go of their own pain; it is too reassuring for them, too comforting. When that happens no matter what you do, you cannot do that for them.

Helping others understand their own value and self worth is an important gift you can offer to your group. In order to assist that process, I offer the following exercises.

~Magickal Connections~

Naming Exercise

THIS IS A WONDERFUL EXERCISE TO GO THROUGH WHEN ONE OF YOUR MEMBERS TAKES A NEW NAME, AND IS ESPECIALLY APPROPRIATE DURING A FULL MOON RITUAL.

HAVE A MEMBER STAND IN THE CENTER OF YOUR CIRCLE. WHILE THE OTHER MEMBERS TAKE TURNS SAYING THAT PERSON'S NAME ALOUD (OR TYPED ON SCREEN, THEN REPEATED AS A CHANT OFFLINE). WHILE CHANTING, EACH MEMBER THEN TAKES A TURN SHARING SOMETHING SPECIAL ABOUT THE PERSON IN THE CIRCLE.

AS AN ALTERNATIVE, WHEN A MEMBER IS TAKING A NEW NAME, HAVE HER/HIM RESEARCH HER/HIS OLD AND NEW NAMES AS MUCH AS POSSIBLE, AND HAVE HER/HIM SHARE THAT RESEARCH WITH THE GROUP AS PART OF HER/HIS RENAMING. HAVE HER/HIM COME UP WITH THREE AFFIRMATIVE STATEMENTS RELATING TO HER/HIS NAME. FOR EXAMPLE, THE NAME LISA COULD HAVE COME FROM ELIZABETH, BUT I CHOOSE TO THINK OF IT AS DERIVING FROM MELISSA. MELISSA DERIVES FROM THE GREEK MELISSAE, WHICH DENOTED A PRIESTESS OF EITHER APHRODITE OR DEMETER. THE AFFIRMATIONS I MIGHT INCORPORATE INTO THE RITUAL MIGHT BE:

I AM LISA, BUSY AS A BEE.[2] I AM LISA, WHOSE BEAUTY IS AN HONOR TO APHRODITE. I AM LISA, WHO BRINGS FORTH BEAUTY INTO THE WORLD!

A Total Healing Bath

TRANSFORM YOUR BATHROOM INTO A SACRED SPACE, ONE FILLED WITH IMAGES, SCENTS, AND OBJECTS THAT MAKE YOU FEEL GOOD. TRY TO INVOLVE EACH OF YOUR SENSES IN A DYNAMIC OF SELF-PLEASURE AND SUPPORT. LIGHT CANDLES ON EVERY AVAILABLE SURFACE; PLAY SOOTHING MUSIC; HAVE A GLASS OF COOL WATER WITH A SQUEEZE OF LEMON OR A BIT OF SUGAR IN IT ON THE COUNTER; TIE A BUNDLE OF CHAMOMILE AND LAVENDER AND LET IT FLOAT IN THE WATER. (I USE A SQUARE OF WOVEN COTTON TIED WITH TWINE WHEN I HAVE LOOSE HERBS RATHER THAN FRESH CUTTINGS.) YOU MAY WANT TO KEEP A PAD OF PAPER NEARBY TO RECORD ANY INFORMATION THAT YOU MAY RECEIVE DURING THIS BATH, AND TO SPREAD IT OUT OVER SEVERAL DAYS. BE GENTLE WITH YOURSELF.

~Maintaining Cohesiveness~

Stand naked and breathe deeply; allow yourself to relax. Out loud, state your intentions for this bath, and ask the God/dess to be with you. Then slip into the water and allow yourself to relax deeper into the warmth of the moment. Breathe deeply and slowly; and let every thought slip away until you are utterly calm and centered.

With your mind, look at yourself. Are there any areas of your body that appear tense or are holding dis-ease? Take a washcloth or a big natural sponge and gently cleanse that area, taking the time to stroke the body part to relaxation, and tell it how much you appreciate its working for you. If you realize that it needs something, remember that thought and do what you can to provide that in the future. Treat your whole body to this cleansing.

Now turn your attention to your mind, to your psyche. Are there places that gape open in your aura? Places where your spirit is diminished? Bathe those places with the healing water, and lovingly stroke them with your astral hands, paying attention to any images or thoughts attached to the wounds. Take your time.

When you are done, relax again into the bathwater. Notice how good it feels to be so strong and healthy— mentally and physically. Take a sip of the water and enjoy the flavor on your tongue. Feel alive. Thank the God/dess for the support and love you feel. Leave the water when you wish, knowing you are stronger and healthier than when you entered.

This bath may be repeated when you desire and is best done during a waxing moon. Feel free to add hot water to keep the temperature up and be prepared to take a long time.

Fear

Another negative aspect that will interfere with cohesion in the circle is fear. Fear takes many forms—some obvious, some subtle—and it may require all of your creative genius to recognize and deal with it. In and of itself, fear is not a negative emotion.

~Magickal Connections~

Fear teaches us many important lessons of survival. We are right to fear the forest fire or to be afraid of a shouting man with a gun. The anger we feel when threatened by politicians arguing to water golf courses at the expense of our salmon arises from fear for our future. The courage we express when fleeing the home we created with a man who beats us is an expression of fear for our lives, or our children's. These are healthy expressions of fear, and the balanced person understands and works with these energies.

But many of us are not so balanced that we recognize the healthy aspects, and instead we support the negative ones. Fear of being undesirable keeps us taking pills or altering our bodies to be beautiful. Fear of being alone convinces us to have sex before we are ready. Fear of causing trouble keeps us silent.

In the circle fear may be expressed as inappropriate anger, or envy. It may come in the form of the member who argues for stability so convincingly, until you realize she is actually trying to create a situation of stagnation. Or perhaps it will be seen in the member whose first reaction to someone questioning him is to bite his/her head off because it feels as though he is being attacked, no matter how benign the questions. Or maybe it will come from the nearly silent member who interacts minimally and reveals little, if anything, about her personal life. Fear can arise almost anywhere.

I offer you these exercises to identify and transform fear in your group. You may wish to have a friend with you while doing them.

Opening the Fear Closet

I DEVELOPED THIS EXERCISE AS A WAY OF LOOKING AT FEAR IN AN OBJECTIVE MANNER. YOU MAY WANT TO HAVE ANOTHER PERSON WITH YOU WHILE YOU GO THROUGH THIS EXERCISE.

~Maintaining Cohesiveness~

GET COMFORTABLE; YOU MAY WISH TO CAST A CIRCLE AND INVITE YOUR SPIRIT GUIDE TO JOIN YOU. STATE ALOUD THAT YOU WISH TO SEE YOUR FEAR AND TO UNDERSTAND IT. BREATHE DEEPLY, RELAX, AND ENTER A DEEP TRANCE STATE.

VISUALIZE YOURSELF IN A SAFE, SACRED PLACE. KNOW THAT YOU ARE VERY STRONG, AND IN THIS PLACE YOUR STRENGTH IS MULTIPLIED TENFOLD. THERE IS A DOOR HERE, WITH A KEY IN THE LOCK. OPEN THE DOOR AND LOOK INSIDE. THAT IS YOUR FEAR.

STANDING IN THE DOORWAY, LOOK AT YOUR FEAR. DOES IT SMELL? IT IS MAKING NOISE?

IT CANNOT CROSS THE THRESHOLD OF THE DOORWAY, SO YOU HAVE PLENTY OF TIME TO LOOK AT IT IN DETAIL. IS IT CONNECTED TO SOMETHING, MAYBE IN THE BACK OF THE CLOSET? LOOK CLOSELY AT THAT CONNECTION AND REMEMBER IT FOR FUTURE CONTEMPLATION.

NAME IT. (NAMING GIVES ONE POWER, AFTER ALL.)

WHEN YOU FEEL YOU HAVE EXAMINED YOUR FEAR LONG ENOUGH, CLOSE THE DOOR.

RETURN TO YOUR BODY SLOWLY AND WITH LOVE.

Breath Transformation[3]

THIS IS NOT AN INTRODUCTORY EXERCISE. USE IT ONLY WHEN YOU ARE READY TO TRANSFORM YOUR FEAR IN A POWERFUL WAY.

CREATE A SACRED SPACE AND INVOKE THE DEITY YOU FEEL A SPECIAL BOND WITH. GET COMFORTABLE. BEGIN TO FOCUS ON YOUR BREATH; BE AWARE OF EACH INHALATION AND EXHALATION. FOLLOW YOUR BREATH INTO YOURSELF, DEEP WITHIN YOUR ATTENTION, YOUR CONSCIOUSNESS. ALLOW YOUR BREATH TO FLOW FREELY AND YOUR MIND TO BECOME STILL.

NOW, TURN YOUR ATTENTION TO YOUR BODY AND LOOK AT WHERE FEAR IS LIVING. IT MAY BE FELT AS TIGHTNESS IN A MUSCLE OR PERHAPS A KNOT OF TENSION. YOU MAY FIND THAT THERE ARE AREAS THAT FEEL "HOT" OR "COLD" OR "ROUGH." CHOOSE ONE AREA TO WORK WITH. BREATHE INTO THAT AREA OF TENSION/FEAR IN YOUR BODY. FEEL THAT AREA EXPAND WITH YOUR BREATH AND THEN CONTRACT IN A RELAXED MANNER AS YOU EXHALE. SOOTHE THE HEAT WITH YOUR COOL BREATH OR MASSAGE IT GENTLY, WHATEVER SEEMS APPROPRIATE. YOUR BREATH IS

~Magickal Connections~

THE KEY: LET IT TRANSFORM THE FEAR INTO ENERGY, WHICH YOU THEN EXHALE OUT OF YOUR BODY. BREATHING, EASE THE TIGHTNESS AND FEEL YOURSELF LOOSENING, DISSOLVING, FLOWING.... REPEAT THROUGH-OUT YOUR BODY.

WHEN YOU ARE FINISHED, OR HAVE DONE AS MUCH AS YOU FEEL YOU CAN, RETURN YOUR ATTENTION TO YOUR BREATH AND ALLOW IT TO RETURN YOU TO PHYSICAL REALITY.

YOU AWAKEN REFRESHED AND LOOSE.

REPEAT AS NEEDED.

Resistance

The third most common hindrance to cohesion in the circle is resistance. Resistance is related to fear, and frequently derives its power from a fear of something (commitment, magick, transformation, change, and so forth).

Perhaps you have a member who always comes late to meetings or rituals, even when you have requested she be on time, or another whose family members seem to always interrupt group sessions. Maybe group members come to circle inebriated or ill-prepared. These are all forms of resistance and can seriously undermine the sense of community you are trying to build within your circle. The most obvious example of this is when members talk inappropriately during ritual. (This is especially troublesome online, where there is no such thing as an offhand comment. Every keystroke is the equivalent of a loudly spoken comment, and it can immediately skew the circle's energies.) There are places and times for unscripted comments during ritual; otherwise it is just plain rude.

Remember the basics of group dynamics (from Chapter 5)? You need to deal with resistance as soon as you recognize it in the circle. Although you probably won't want to deal with resistance in public, it may be necessary. If so, remember that the resistant member may not be aware of causing a disruption. (This is especially true of newcomers to the Craft.) Using talking during ritual as an example, gently remind the group that this is a sacred moment. Perhaps say, "Everyone, focus," to bring the attention back to the moment.

Other situations can probably be dealt with via a frank discussion. Be honest and firm, and, if possible, allow the resistant member to come to his own awareness of the disruption. The lesson is much more likely to be acted upon if he sees the issue for himself and acts on it.

One way to open up and get over one's resistance to something is to literally act in an open and generous manner. The following exercise will do that.

Blessings for a Day

THE ACT OF BLESSING SOMEONE IS A POWERFUL WAY TO CONNECT WITH THE DIVINE WITHIN EACH OF US. OUR SOCIETY RECOGNIZES THIS IN THE FORM OF THE MAGICKAL INCANTATION "BLESS YOU" EVOKED AFTER SOMEONE SNEEZES. WITH THIS EXERCISE, WE GO A STEP FURTHER.

FOR EACH ACTION YOU PERFORM THROUGHOUT A DAY, OBSERVE THE ACTION AND SAY A BLESSING. THE BLESSING CAN BE SILENT OR VOCALIZED. FOR EXAMPLE, WHILE YOU ARE BRUSHING YOUR TEETH, YOU MIGHT SAY, "BLESS MY TEETH THAT THEY REMAIN STRONG AND HEALTHY." PERHAPS YOU MIGHT SAY A BLESSING FOR THE FARMERS AND OTHER PROVIDERS OF THE FOOD YOU EAT AT BREAKFAST. IF A CO-WORKER IS HAVING A BAD DAY, SAY A BLESSING FOR HER. EACH ENCOUNTER, EACH ACTIVITY IS A PLACE FOR A BLESSING. ACKNOWLEDGE THAT MOMENT AS A CONNECTION WITH THE DIVINE.

THIS EXERCISE IS MOST POWERFUL WHEN YOU BLESS EVERY ACTION, REVEALING THE NEED AND OPPORTUNITY FOR BLESSING IN OUR LIVES.

~Magickal Connections~

Creating Cohesiveness

Cohesiveness is a vital part of a magickal group's successful existence, and it is fragile. Mundane life will always interfere with participation, and unless its members actively work to maintain their bonds, the magickal group will dry up and blow away. It is important that all group members realize the role of their personal responsibility in creating and maintaining cohesiveness. A naturally withdrawn person, one who prefers to have others ask if there are problems, will have to work much harder to maintain a sense of community. Most especially, it is not possible to see a person withdraw online, nor can the need to be reached toward. Members who need must do some reaching themselves.

Here are some general ideas for encouraging cohesiveness.

Do Ritual

RITUAL, NO MATTER HOW SMALL OR SIMPLE, IS A POWERFUL WAY TO BUILD COMMUNITY. EACH TIME YOU WORK TOGETHER MAGICKALLY, YOU ADD TO THE "GROUP MIND" AND THE DYNAMICS OF THE GROUP'S STRUCTURE.

Encourage Storytelling

THE BEST WAY TO DO THIS IS TO SHARE STORIES FROM YOUR OWN LIFE, OR THINGS THAT INFLUENCE YOU. THE RAINBOW YOU SAW THIS MORNING, THE FUNNY THING YOUR BABY DID LAST NIGHT, EVEN THAT SILLY MISTAKE YOU MADE LAST YEAR. MORE SPECIFICALLY, IF YOUR GROUP INTERACTS DAILY (ONLINE, FOR EXAMPLE) I RECOMMEND HAVING DAILY MEDITATIONS IN WHICH A NEW PERSON TAKES HER/HIS TURN EACH WEEK AT POSTING TEXT OR GRAPHICS THAT S/HE FEELS ARE NOTEWORTHY. IN MY GROUPS WE HAVE SEEN QUOTES RANGING FROM THE WORLD'S PHILOSOPHERS TO HEAVY METAL SONG LYRICS, INCLUDING PASSAGES FROM BOOKS AND ESSAYS ON HOW TO ORGANIZE YOUR LIFE. THE PHOTOS

~Maintaining Cohesiveness~

HAVE RANGED FROM A HILARIOUS SERIES OF "ANTI-MOTIVATION" POSTERS THROUGH COMPUTER ARTWORK, TO THE PAINTINGS OF MASTERS AND PERSONAL PHOTOGRAPHS.

Pen Pals

RANDOMLY ASSIGN PAIRS OF MEMBERS FOR A MONTH. ENCOURAGE THEM TO WRITE TO ONE ANOTHER DIRECTLY, SHARE STORIES, AND JUST "HANG OUT" ON THEIR OWN TIME. PARTICIPATION IS UP TO THEM, BUT ENCOURAGED. THIS SHOULD ENCOURAGE PERSONAL BONDING WITHIN THE MAGICKAL GROUP.

Buddy System

DIVIDE A LARGE GROUP (ONE WITH MORE THAN 13 MEMBERS) INTO SMALLER GROUPS, HEADED BY AN ELDER; INCLUDE THE LEADER IN EACH GROUP. EACH MEMBER (A BUDDY) PAYS ATTENTION TO THE OTHERS IN HIS/HER GROUP, MAKING SURE EVERYTHING IS OKAY. THIS ALLOWS SHY MEMBERS TO BE DRAWN OUT A BIT MORE, AND IF A MEMBER IS FEELING DEPRESSED AND/OR ALONE, A FRIENDLY "ARE YOU OKAY?" CAN RELIVE THE BURDEN. (A BONUS TO THIS IDEA IS THAT THESE "BUDDY GROUPS" CAN FORM THE NUCLEUS FOR FUTURE GROUPS.)

CHAPTER 9

CONFRONTING CONFLICT

The purpose of conflict is conflict resolution, and we've found that when people are treated well in conflict, it makes a tremendous contribution to establishing order.

—*Lt. Colonel James Brown of the U.S. Army*[1]

The ugly side of politics has probably existed since the first meeting of more than three people. What is sad about it is that, although you might expect fewer ugly political issues in a spiritually focused group, that is not often the case. Negative politics can be subtle. Then again, they can easily be explosive.

Natural Antagonists

Magickal groups end, sometimes spectacularly. At times, this is simply a natural part of the process of creation and dissolution (see Chapter 7 for more on the life cycle of a magickal group). But when a group has dissolved with anger and pain and disillusion on all sides, and especially when hindsight reveals that everyone was using good strategies for communicating and attempting to understand, it's time to look for another answer. The incredibly destructive breakdowns, the ones that rip magickal groups apart, the conflicts that result in broken spirits, are not accidents. Nor are they the consequence of simple misunderstandings or miscommunications. They happen because specific individuals make them happen.

Magick attracts a wide variety of people, and some of them are only interested in building up their own personal power and supporting their self image. These people are the troublemakers in every magickal group and, although they are not easy to spot in the beginning, they inevitably show their true selves. Antagonists frequently are unaware of the damage they are causing. That's one reason they are so hard to find: They aren't cackling with glee and twirling their mustaches. In fact, they're some of the ones rushing to staunch the bleeding. Their defining characteristic is that they need conflict, and they are superb at turning even simple encounters into situations of manipulation and defensive posturing.

A personal example came from the first year of my old coven, ShadowMoon. One of the members was a well-known member of the online community, a (self-proclaimed) 3rd Degree who was the owner and administrator of the e-mail list that was the genesis of ShadowMoon. I will call her Lady Catfish. Our High Priestess asked her to act as the Handmaiden with specific duties, and the offer was enthusiastically accepted. Lady Catfish did not fulfill her role, and essentially was a nonmember. Finally, the High Priestess called her and pointed out that she was letting the coven down and had to get her act together. Unbeknownst to the High Priestess, Lady Catfish arranged to have the call monitored by a third party, and guided the call in such a way that the High Priestess revealed confidential information. The third party then published the information to the coven (as "proof" that the High Priestess was wrong and Lady Catfish was right). Our trust was shattered, our sense of safety obliterated. Several members left over the situation, and it was devastating.

Defusing Antagonists

There is a simple technique to use when you encounter a natural antagonist: Ask them to leave, and don't let them back. I know that seems harsh, but please remember: These people thrive on crisis, and, as long as they are a part of your group, crisis is the only thing that will be present. It's similar to firing someone in that you don't have to explain yourself. (Or, as a friend once counseled me before I had to fire an employee, "every word just means a longer deposition.") A straightforward "I don't think you are working out in our group; there are other places you will fit in better" is enough. You may be asked to explain, but remember: This person thrives on the energy of dispute. S/he doesn't want an answer (s/he probably knows the answer); s/he wants an argument.

Difficult People

When we encounter difficult people, it is helpful to remember three things:

- ◉ Random encounters are rarely random.
- ◉ The pain and frustration we experience with these people are just as important for our personal growth as love and exploration.
- ◉ When we work with these people and heal our relationships with them (transform them from difficult), we are engaging in a transformative experience that changes not only ourselves but our view and experience of the world.

In dealing with difficult people, we are reminded to not assume that our perspective is the truth. It may be that their nature arises from personal circumstances (unstable work situation, abusive relationship, changing family dynamic). It may also be that they are difficult because we have unfinished business regarding this dynamic. For example, I have a hard time working with passive/aggressive people. That particular personality dynamic sets my teeth on edge and makes me crazy. My ability to work with them was positively changed, however, when I realized that their behavior reminded me of a difficult time in my life with my mother. Just the realization that my reaction was coming from a long-hidden event opened me up to having more compassion in dealing with passive/aggressive people, and, therefore, eased the relationships.

Negative experiences do not mean that your life is bad—that is a subjective and somewhat immature perspective. Having a wonderful life, with no pain, or suffering, or tears, sounds very nice on paper, but it probably isn't healthy. Even the serene Buddhist monks regularly take on and fully experience the world's suffering in their practice—not because they are masochists, but because they need to experience it to understand it and heal it through compassion. In your own life, have you ever been positively transformed by being happy? By suffering? Difficult moments bring enormous spiritual benefit and many lessons for us to encompass, not only about ourselves, but also about our relationships, our place within the world, and about the Divine.

The only thing we can truly change about a negative person is our reaction to them. How we respond is our choice, entirely. Such a powerful position that is for us—how daunting it can be to have such power!

So, the first question to ask is this: What is the potential lesson here? In doing so, you cultivate the habit of reserving judgment. After you have the facts you may still choose to view the person as difficult, but perhaps the facts will instead open your understanding to a new perspective. This new perspective may provide greater understanding, or perhaps just a new view of old terrain, but in either case it provides you with more opportunities to respond and more choices of how to respond when you do so.

Remember that how we perceive something—a person, an event—informs how we feel about it. Gladiolas make me happy, but they are funeral flowers to my mother, so she feels sad when she sees them. Difficult people are the same way. Our perception of them as difficult places them into a negative context, but our reactions to them can be turned around so that they become positive experiences instead. A birth is a difficult, painful process, but the process has its own joys (and endorphins) so that we welcome it rather than fear it. Difficult people have the capacity to become our greatest teachers because they provoke reactions in us that we can use as signposts to our inner resources and landscape. That which we fear teaches us power.

Everyone, every encounter, offers an opportunity to learn. Being open to the possibility is the first step. Think of the universe as a huge schoolroom with planned curriculums and surprise agendas from visiting professors. We have optional courses and required curricula that we may or may not complete. Some classes are so easy for us it seems we're remembering knowledge we already had; other classes we fail and have to re-take until we get a passing grade. I don't want to belabor this analogy, but the hardest classes are likely the ones we pay the most attention to, and learn the most from. The tests are often subtle, and usually presented as a choice we must make. A self-centered person may find himself caring for an elderly relative, and in so doing realize the value of another is equal to his own. A painfully shy person might find herself in a unique situation to speak up on behalf of an absent friend and discover that the passion that inflamed her to speak for another has warmed her ability to speak for herself as well.

~Magickal Connections~

I have a Zen alarm clock. At the hour the alarm it is set for, a quiet chime is struck. Five minutes later that chime is struck again, and then at two minutes. The chimes increase in frequency until it is chiming constantly (and loudly) for five minutes, and then they taper off until the next day. The universe presents lessons the way my alarm clock does: The first opportunity is quiet and unobtrusive, but later ones are louder and more insistent. For those of us who really lack all subtlety there is the Cosmic 2 x 4 that whacks us upside the head. That's the most painful situation of all.

Throughout the test, life is painful, confusing, and difficult. It is rare that we can see how anything positive will manifest, even if we are an incurable optimist. We might have faith that it will be worthwhile, but we don't *know*. Not until it's over, and we are given the perspective to see the journey and understand the value of the gift we were granted. That insight can act as the fuel for the next stage of our journey and as a balm for the spiritual buffeting we just endured.

Writing It Out

AFTER YOU'VE HAD AN ENCOUNTER WITH A DIFFICULT PERSON, TAKE THE TIME TO WRITE WRITE DOWN YOUR FEELINGS. DESCRIBE THE SITUATION AS BEST YOU CAN AND THEN DESCRIBE YOUR REACTIONS, DESIRES, AND ACTIONS TO THAT SITUATION. FANTASIZE AND SHARE THAT; PLAY OUT SCENARIOS; DOCUMENT YOUR ACTIONS. BY WRITING, WE TAKE WHAT IS INSIDE AND FLING IT OUT TO PONDER, OBSERVE, AND REARRANGE. IT CAN BE HEALING AS IT PURGES US OF PAINFUL FEELINGS, SHOWS US A PIECE OF A PATTERN, OR REVEALS HITHERTO UNHEARD TAPES FROM OUR PAST. WRITING CAN ALSO (BUT NOT AT THE SAME TIME) SERVE AS A FORM OF COMMUNICATION TO THE OTHER. EVEN IF THEY NEVER SEE THE DOCUMENT, IT WILL HAVE SERVED A PURPOSE FOR YOU IN CREATING THE IDEAL DIALOGUE.

Emotional Body Awareness

DO THE FOLLOWING MEDITATION TO LEARN ABOUT THE BODY AWARENESS WE BRING TO VARIOUS EMOTIONAL SITUATIONS.

~Confronting Conflict~

GET COMFORTABLE. RELAX AS DEEPLY AS YOU CAN AND BRING YOUR AWARENESS TO YOUR BREATHING. FOCUS—IN AN EASY, RELAXED WAY—ON YOUR BREATHING. RELAX COMPLETELY.

THINK OF A PERSON WHO LOVES YOU DEEPLY. LET THAT PERSON COME INTO YOUR AWARENESS AND NOTICE HOW YOUR BODY FEELS. YOU MAY FEEL A SENSE OF LIGHTNESS, A PHYSICAL JOY. OR AN EXPANSION IN YOUR HEAD (OR CHEST). PAY ATTENTION TO WHAT YOU NOTICE, AND LOOK FOR ALL SIGNS OF REACTION TO BEING LOVED.

WHEN YOU FEEL YOU HAVE LEARNED ALL YOU CAN (THIS MAY TAKE SEVERAL SESSIONS), REPEAT IT; BUT THIS TIME THINK ABOUT SOMEONE WHO UPSETS YOU. THIS IS LIKELY TO BE DIFFICULT, BUT CAN TEACH YOU A GREAT DEAL. NOTICE HOW YOUR BODY SHIFTS AND CHANGES, AND WHAT YOU FEEL (AND WHERE) WHEN YOU THINK OF THIS PERSON AND THE UNPLEASANTNESS ASSOCIATED WITH THEM. (TRY NOT TO GET CAUGHT UP IN PLAYING OUT SCENARIOS, BUT FOCUS ON JUST HOW YOU FEEL WHEN YOU THINK ABOUT THEM.) DOES YOUR BREATHING CHANGE? DO MUSCLES TIGHTEN? (WHICH ONES, AND HOW?)

ALLOW THIS PERSON TO LEAVE YOUR AWARENESS. SAY GOODBYE TO HIM/HER AND RETURN TO A NEUTRAL STATE. FOCUSING ONCE AGAIN ON BREATHING EASILY WILL HELP EASE ANY STRESS. FINISH WHEN YOU ARE ONCE AGAIN RELAXED.

AS A VARIATION OF THE ABOVE:

KEEP A JOURNAL OF THE PAINFUL SITUATION AND DOCUMENT THE DAILY EVENTS, REACTIONS, AND PROGRESS (IF ANY) YOU FEEL AND SEE ALONG THE WAY. BY DOING SO YOU OFFER YOURSELF THE OPPORTUNITY TO FIND INSIGHT IN THE MIDST OF THE PROCESS, A SAFE SPACE TO RECORD YOUR FEELINGS WITHOUT FEAR OF BACKLASH, AND A PLACE TO SEE HOW YOU HAVE CHANGED, EVEN IF THE DIFFICULT PERSON DOES NOT.

Clarify Your Goals

BEFORE MEETING WITH SOMEONE WHO CAUSES YOU PAIN, DO THIS EXERCISE TO HELP IDENTIFY WHAT YOU WANT FROM THE ENCOUNTER.

FIRST, WRITE OUT THE SPECIFIC, TANGIBLE THINGS OR BEHAVIORS YOU WANT. THIS CAN BE ANYTHING FROM DOLLAR AMOUNTS TO ACTIONS.

SECOND, WRITE OUT HOW YOU WANT THE RELATIONSHIP TO CHANGE. IS YOUR DESIRE TO GROW CLOSER, OR HAVE MORE DISTANCE

BETWEEN THE TWO OF YOU? PERHAPS THERE NEEDS TO BE A SHIFT IN HOW DECISIONS ARE MADE.?

THIRD, WRITE OUT YOUR EMOTIONAL GOALS. HOW DO YOU WANT TO FEEL AFTER THIS ENCOUNTER? TRIUMPHANT? FREE? DO YOU NEED AN ADMISSION OF GUILT, OR AN APOLOGY?

FOURTH, WRITE OUT ANY PROCESS-RELATED ITEMS YOU WANT TO HAVE FOLLOWED. PERHAPS A CONTRACT NEEDS TO BE DRAWN UP? OR SPECIFIC AGREEMENTS MADE ABOUT FUTURE CONTACT?

FINALLY, REVIEW YOUR GOALS AND ASSIGN THEM A MEASURE OF IMPORTANCE IN RELATION TO ONE ANOTHER. THE PAYING OF THE DEBT (MATERIAL) MIGHT BE FAR MORE IMPORTANT THAN RECEIVING AN APOLOGY (EMOTIONAL), FOR EXAMPLE. AS YOU ARE DOING THIS, CONSIDER WHAT YOU ARE WILLING TO GIVE UP TO ACHIEVE YOUR GOALS AND CONSIDER ALTERNATIVES THAT MIGHT STILL BE VIABLE SOLUTIONS.

Ordinary Conflict

Ordinary conflict in groups happens when individuals believe they are not getting what they need or want, and are protecting their own self-interest. Sometimes the individual is not conscious of the need and is acting without awareness. Other times, the individual is actively working to achieving a goal. Keeping in mind that conflict is inevitable, we can take comfort in knowing that there are early warning signals and strategies for resolution that absolutely work.

Conflict generally arises from poor communication between group members. It may also arise when there is a sense of dissatisfaction with group leadership, management style, or a feeling that secrets are being kept. It may also come about during a change in leadership. It can also happen organically. I caution readers to not rush to judgment but to allow the situation to develop and provide further information (as we do with difficult people).

~Confronting Conflict~

Early warning signals of conflict are:

- Disagreements, regardless of issue.
- Withholding bad news.
- Strong public statements.
- Conflicts in value system.
- Increasing lack of respect.
- Open disagreement.
- Lack of candor on sensitive issues.
- Lack of clear goals.

I believe that conflict can be good for a group if it is managed appropriately. By airing differences, group members can engender self-empowerment, positive growth, and satisfying interpersonal relationships. Constructive conflict can produce better ideas, new approaches, and a higher level of creativity. It can force people to see, and deal with, previously hidden problems.

Destructive conflict, however, takes attention away from other important activities, undermines morale, and polarizes people.

Mitigating Conflict

There are several strategies for dealing with conflict: (Some or all may be appropriate at any point during the process of resolution.)

- Meet conflict head on. As distasteful as it is, stepping to meet it gives you a little more space to move around in.
- Set goals. What is the "win-win" answer?
- Be honest about concerns on both sides.
- Allow "agreement to disagree." To a minimum degree it's okay not to resolve every point

immediately. But understand that even minor disagreements can be detrimental, and should be dealt with at some point.

 Keep your ego out of the discussion. If a group member doesn't like how something is done, that's not necessarily a slight on you or anyone else.

 Discuss differences in values openly.

If you are a leader in your group and are directly involved in the dispute, you may want to ask for a mediator. Sometimes a mediator can create a more productive discussion than the disputing parties could have had by themselves. To do this, mediators help the parties determine facts, show empathy and impartiality with the parties, and help the parties generate new ideas.

Salt Water Cleansing

TAKE A BOWL OF CLEAR, FRESH WATER. BREATHE ACROSS THE SURFACE AND SAY, "BLESSED BE." SPRINKLE SALT INTO THE WATER AND STIR CLOCKWISE UNTIL DISSOLVED, BREATHE ACROSS THE SURFACE AGAIN, AND SAY, "BLESSED BE." LIGHT A CANDLE WITH THE WORDS "MAY I BE CLEANSED," AND PROCEED TO DRAIN ALL OF THE NEGATIVITY OUT OF YOU AND INTO THE WATER. TALK IT OUT, SHOUT IT OUT, DANCE, CRY, OR SING— WHATEVER AND HOWEVER SPIRIT MOVES YOU TO RELEASE THE NEGATIVITY.

WHEN YOU ARE THROUGH, SPEND AS LONG AS YOU WISH IN THE PERFECT SAFETY OF THE CLEANSING. THEN, USING YOUR INDEX FINGER, STIR THE WATER COUNTER-CLOCKWISE SAYING, "AS ABOVE, SO BELOW. THE INNER BECOMES THE OUTER." WHEN THE WATER FEELS CLEANSED AGAIN, SAY, "BLESSED BE" AND POUR IT DOWN THE DRAIN.

Healthy Self-Doubt

A magickal group member who never questions his or her own actions and decisions is a fool. On the other hand, a group participant who allows self-doubt to thwart effective and necessary action is equally a fool. The constant reexamination of one's beliefs and understanding of issues is a healthy behavior pattern. I suggest this: Don't assume you're right, but don't refuse to make decisions just because you might be wrong.

Magickal group leaders are responsible for the health of the group and must take the steps necessary to protect it. Group members rely on them to do this; the power to do so is given gladly. (Knowing this makes it a bit easier to see why the dreaded "High Priestess Disease"[2] is so prevalent among younger witches.) The solution to getting past indecision is to have frequent discussions within your magickal group about conflict, so that they understand the issues as well as you do. They can offer their own valuable perspectives, and together you can discuss strategies for dealing with conflict—before it arises.

Anger Within the Circle

The face of conflict that is least easy to deal with is that of anger. Anger can be a very healthy and purifying force in our lives. Anger shows us what we fear or where we are unhappy with a situation. It can be a wonderful release and a positive life-changer. More often than not, however, anger acts as a festering wound on our psyche, one that oozes pain and creates disruption in our lives. For many people, being angry is the force that motivates us, giving us the strength to survive in a difficult life. Being angry may be the only time we feel truly alive and strong. Anger can be a two-bladed sword, however, with one blade cutting outward into others, and the other slicing into the wielder.

In the circle, anger can act the way a forest fire does, destroying and raging out of control, or it may act as the catalyst for change, clearing the old and stagnant to make way for new growth. All along that spectrum, anger is a powerful force that may go from destructive to creative in an instant, and is always difficult for the group to handle.

Many women come to witchcraft because they feel betrayed at the lack of validation they receive from traditional religions. That feeling of betrayal can easily change to anger not only at the religion itself but also at the men who perpetuate it, and from there into men in general. One of my members had an extremely negative experience as a young girl with her local church, which changed pastors from a tolerant "let girls serve at the altar" preacher to a preacher who believed that "girls are full of sin and not worthy to serve the Lord." For her, more than a decade later, this experience was proof that all traditional religions and anything God-oriented was bad, and anything Goddess-oriented was good. We spent more than a year discussing this situation, to no avail, and she eventually left our dual deity coven to find one more suited to her needs. She just could not let go of her anger and it colored too much of her interactions with other members. We understood that this was likely a stage in the evolution of her Self, but it was disruptive for a circle that includes men.

Self-depreciation, anger's ugly underside, is much more pervasive. The person who says, "I know this is a stupid question" is expressing anger—at himself—for not knowing the answer. So is the person who consistently apologizes for being "such a problem" over minor inconsequential matters. For this kind of person, anger has gone from fiery to icy; it has moved to the opposite end of the spectrum and might be seen as a form of depression.

Then there are my favorite angry people: those who are passive/aggressive in their personalities. These are the people who are unhappy, but do not say anything directly about the cause of their displeasure. One of our founding coven members had been gradually withdrawing over a period of a year

until her participation was next to non-existent. It came to a head when she ignored several direct messages I sent to her asking for information about what was going on. Finally, the High Priestess stepped in and sent her a message telling her to call collect but to contact her immediately. She did not and so, a day later, we removed her from the list (and therefore the coven). She sent us an angry, vicious message bemoaning the group's decline into "just a list" where "no one has any connection to anyone else," unlike the early days when we were a "real" community. We all thought this was interestingly misguided of her. How could she feel connected to a community in which she did not participate?

Anger is an extraordinary emotion, bred into us through evolution as an effective survival mechanism. Anger is the effect of another's encroachment into our territory (and therefore depletion of our resources) and leads to our fighting back. Anger keeps us from being stepped on by others and put down. We are no longer living in a "simple resources = safety" environment, but, instead, in a complex world of interaction and reaction. Here, anger is still a valuable and informative emotion, but it must be balanced by judgment; we must merge our civilized selves' power of judgment with our primitive selves' emotion. We must be able to judge when to express our anger as well as in what fashion and to what degree. Someone taking the last donut may provoke anger in us, but we must decide whether its really worth getting emotional over it, or if a mild remark would be more appropriate. Reacting to being passed over for a promotion is rarely a good thing to do in public, although the angry feeling can be very intense.

The Dalai Lama says that "anger cannot be overcome by anger" and suggests that meeting another's anger with compassion, tolerance, and patience will diffuse the other's anger while maintaining your own peace. It is a lovely ideal, but difficult to achieve. Many of us have issues with anger arising from such sources as childhood training (or its lack) or personal relationships, even chemical imbalances. Nonetheless, the consequences of unrestrained anger are visible and severe, affecting both the person expressing the anger and those on the receiving end. Coming to terms with our anger is a profoundly important task in our spiritual development.

Earth Blood

GET COMFORTABLE, RELAX, AND FOLLOW YOUR BREATH INTO A TRANCE STATE. FEEL YOUR SPINE GROW ROOTS; WITH EACH BREATH THE ROOTS GROW AND BURROW INTO THE EARTH. DEEPER IN AND STILL DEEPER THE ROOTS GROW UNTIL THE REACH THE EARTH'S BLOOD—THE LAVA. THE ROOTS PLUNGE INTO THE LAVA AND ITS ENERGY—NOT BURNING BUT WARM—FLOWS INTO YOU. DRINK OF THE LAVA'S ENERGY UNTIL YOU ARE FULL UP, BRIMMING WITH LIFE FORCE.

NOW, REMEMBER A TIME WHEN YOU WERE ANGRY. RECALL THE EMOTION, THE PASSION YOU FELT AT THAT TIME. HOW DID YOU EXPRESS IT? VERBALLY? PHYSICALLY? DID YOU REPRESS IT AND PRETEND IT WAS NOT THERE? NOTE WHERE IN YOUR BODY THAT ANGER RESIDES—IN YOUR CLENCHED JAW, PERHAPS, OR IN YOUR BACK, EVEN IN YOUR STOMACH.

RELEASE THE IMAGES, THE MEMORY OF YOUR ANGER, BUT RETAIN THE SENSATION IN YOUR BODY. USE THE ENERGY OF THE LAVA TO SOOTHE AND RELAX THE ANGER, TRANSFORMING IT INTO NOURISHMENT. TRANSFORM ALL THE ANGER AND ITS SENSATIONS INTO LAVA ENERGY.

RECALL AGAIN THE ANGRY SITUATION CLEARLY. ASK YOURSELF HOW YOU MIGHT HAVE FELT OR ACTED DIFFERENTLY HAD YOU BEEN GROUNDED, AS YOU ARE NOW, IN THE EARTH'S ENERGY? AVOID SELF-RECRIMINATION OR BLAME. RE-CREATE THE SCENE FROM THE PERSPECTIVE OF BEING GROUNDED AND FULL OF EARTH ENERGY. SEE YOUR ANGER TRANSFORMED INTO RIGHT ACTION, EACH ACTION CLEAR AND HARMONIOUS.

~Confronting Conflict~

Breathe out and release the images. Relax and release the lava, return the roots into yourself. As you breathe, say, "I am connected to the Earth." You return relaxed, refreshed, and full of energy.

Anger is way to get attention and is valuable when used to draw attention to injustice, abuses of power, inequities, and other negative group dynamic situations. Anger can teach you about what you are afraid of, and how much (or little) power you have. It can give you the strength to change your world, as it did some of the greatest humanitarians. Anger also arises from unfulfilled desires, and, although we can't always get what we want, we should be able to get what we need; anger can show us our unfulfilled needs and open us to ways to satisfy those needs.

To achieve balance with our anger, we begin by examining what kind of anger might be appropriate to express and how the expression of anger might be controlled so that it is a tool of communication rather than a dangerous force.

Exercises for Dealing With Anger

Begin to pay attention to how your body feels when you are angry. Perhaps your back tenses, your head pounds, or maybe you just feel a tightening of the chest. By tracking the bodily sensations of how it feels to be angry you can begin to notice the early signs of anger, and manage that anger and control it. (Please also see the Earth Blood exercise on page 162.)

Whenever possible, express your anger to the person responsible for it once you have calmed down. Phrase this conversation in "I" terms ("I was angry about X" instead of "You made me angry when you did Y") and describe the behavior that triggered the anger.

~Magickal Connections~

I have found that an excellent way to work with anger is to understand it as a kind of energy. Many of us have leftover "voices" in our heads from our upbringing, telling us that anger is "bad" or that it will destroy us if we express it. Some will have reversed those messages and may think "anger is good," or "I need to be angry in order to change." Either way makes anger a kind of place to be, rather than a form of power, of energy, that we can utilize and control.

Depression Can Be Healthy

When we enter a period of intense growth we experience radical or frequent changes in our life. It is as if, having decided that we want to grow, the Universe requires that we get rid of many old habits, patterns, and beliefs to make room. It is inevitable. Sometimes this process is one of joy, even when it is difficult (we give up smoking, or watching television, or our solitary life). More often than not, however, it is painful because we give up things that we love (or at least a part of ourselves for a long time, and therefore familiar). When we give up those things, we open the door to depression. This emotion has been given a very bad reputation in the last several decades. Given a casual look at a major magazine, particularly those aimed at families and women, you might think that depression is the root cause for everything wrong in life (followed closely by lack of sleep). But depression can be a valid and healthy emotion when it arises as part of an effective mourning period for that which you have given up. It is nurturing and healing to withdraw from the busy stream of life and soak in an eddy for a period. To my mind, faking being happy when you are undergoing a radical change is more damaging than feeling depressed.

A dear friend and covenmate of mine was depressed for years, which seems to be a long time until you know what she was going through, among them her mother's deteriorating mental and physical health, her husband's transgender issues, a major relocation, and her own sleep and health issues. For her, being depressed for a long period of time was a necessary part of adjusting to the changes and finding her new level of "normal."

Depression can be healing—a necessary process of mourning that which you are giving up or undergoing. In an unbalanced person it can also be debilitating. For me, it has been both. Debilitating depression comes to me when I feel burdened by the choices I see. Instinctively, I see that the choices are not healthy or they require more courage than I believe I possess. Knowledge is a burden and my instinctive response is depression, a conscious turning away and putting off of the choice. In some cases, the opportunity passes me by and I remain in the same place (which can also produce depression, of course). In others, the possibility of change waits, as though a plant dormant in winter, until my acceptance of it activates it and causes it to bloom. I am rarely aware that this is the case. I only feel bewildered and unhappy. As do many people who go into therapy, I find myself saying, "I have no idea why I am depressed." This is not deliberately disingenuous of me, but, even though my unconscious knows what is going on, my conscious self has not taken the time to examine the situation. In fact, when I begin to move out of depression (a process that can take weeks of gradually "lightening" in my outlook, or happen seemingly overnight) it is because I have begun to listen to my unconscious and shift my perspective to accommodate the new information.

The most serious case of depression I have undergone took place several years ago, and the cause was the ending of a deeply passionate and utterly doomed love relationship. I had given up so much of my self in the relationship (one reason it was doomed, of course) that its ending came, quixotically, as a relief. At the same time, however, I had to give up the years of dreams, fantasies, and desires that I had built in to the relationship. I functioned "normally," and few people had any idea of the true state of my sadness for nearly a year. I only began to heal from the loss when I started to examine the relationship from a perspective of "how much did I expect?" instead of "how much I lost!" It took another year of trance work, journaling, and (eventually) talking about my loss with others before I could forgive my former lover for not fulfilling my expectations. My depression lasted into that second year, gradually fading away until, one day, it was simply gone. My mourning was over and I could place my grief into perspective.

Loss is a part of life, and frequently mark periods of transition; it is one reason many witchcraft traditions use the metaphor of death/rebirth to symbolize initiation. You are dying in the old life to become a new being. The process of transition requires that we give up the old comfortable ways and cherished beliefs to grow, and this is painful. Being told "don't cling" does not really help someone who is not ready to hear that message, just as the message "don't be sad; this is a great opportunity" is just plain silly. We do not mourn those things that did not matter to us; we mourn that which we cared for the most. Maturity (which marks not age, but growth) requires that we understand our selves well enough that we welcome the vagaries of life with joy and attention, placing them within context of our personal knowledge, and yet allowing each to be itself—unique and valued for its uniqueness.

When we accept that we will feel loss, accept that we will suffer in life, the pain of loss lessens and it becomes a teacher, a companion, rather than an enemy. When you were a child, matters that were of deep importance and pain were all-consuming. Those very same matters are less consequential as an adult. The matters did not change. You did, by growing up and maturing.

When to Walk Away

Magickal groups must be aware of the use and misuse of power when only a small group is in control—not just in the classic sense of having a leader who must control everything, but in subtle ways as well. For example, you create a magickal group, and ask your best friend to join you and share her knowledge. She (a longtime witch with decades of experience) enthusiastically agrees and immediately begins to hold classes and do rituals. Suddenly, you don't have as much to do. A few months go by, and some asks, "Whose group is it?" In this case, an honest discussion between you and her will probably clear up the issue, at least for the two of you, but maybe not for the rest of the magickal group. Because even if you deliberately set out to equalize the power, it requires ongoing awareness and attention to keep it balanced.

A trusting, safe environment, where intimacy is nurtured but not forced, and sharing is spontaneous and loving, produces a magickal group of extraordinary strength and power. For this reason, a magickal group is frequently likened to a family. There is a mother and a father (the High Priestess and

~Magickal Connections~

Priest), older relations (the Elders), and younger siblings (the whole magickal group). Squabbles happen, but they are dealt with generously, and misunderstandings are quickly solved and forgotten. The magickal group becomes the place members turn to for love and support and where they receive it immediately. The deepest trust is built out of the conflicts we resolve, for how can we know the strength of the structure we have built until it is tested in the scary, nerve-wracking crucible of strife?

Some warning signs of a magickal group "gone bad" or being subsumed by negative politics are apathy, lack of participation, low attendance at rituals, promises broken, gossip, back-stabbing, and flames. If you find yourself in a magickal group where any of these things are the norm, walk away. It is not worth your energy to try to fix the situation. Remember that leaving in anger will not help—either the magickal group or you—so just leave. If you absolutely must say something, just be brief and to the point, and remember that your words may come back to haunt you.

There are general ways of dealing with nasty politics and conflict. They are not always the easiest guidelines to remember, but they do work in almost any circumstance.

1. Use "I" statements when talking about your concerns. "I" takes responsibility for your feelings. Using "you" statements sound accusing or judging the other person.
2. Speak from your heart; say how you feel. Feelings are valuable and vital, and they cannot be denied.
3. Be clear about how you feel before you speak. It may be necessary to separate your feelings about the person, or the manner in which the issue was presented, from how you actually feel about the issue.

~Confronting Conflict~

4. Deal with the issue in the most appropriate place. If someone says something rude to you, don't respond in public. Take her/him aside and discuss it privately.

5. Deal with the issue as soon as possible. Do not let time pass before you contact the source; your anger will grow and fester. As well, the more time that passes, the more likely it will be that the originator will have forgotten the context of the situation, or what was said.

In the end, what makes conflict rewarding is the willingness of everyone involved to resolve the issue and learn from the experience.

If your group has succumbed to nasty group dynamics, you face a very difficult task: Do you leave or close it down? Or try to transform the negativity into a better situation? Only you can make that decision, but I hope the tools I have given you here help.

Recognizing Choice

It is often said that a witch's will is her most powerful tool. This visualization will assist you in clarifying your will, particularly in difficult situations.

Cast your circle and create sacred space. Invoke Athena and Mars and ask Their assistance in seeing the situation clearly so as to make a decision. Get comfortable and follow your breath in to a trance state.

You find yourself in your sacred space, your personal astral temple. A reflecting pool is at its center, lit by the temple's candles and the light of the moon high overhead. Make your way to the pool and drink from its purity. Feel the cool water flow through you. Kneel at the water's edge and breathe deeply until you are calm and centered.

~Magickal Connections~

LOOK DEEP INTO THE POOL AND SAY ALOUD, "LET ME SEE (_THE SITUATION_) CLEARLY, WITHOUT EMOTION." WATCH AS IMAGES FORM AND DISSOLVE ON THE WATER'S SURFACE, TELLING YOU THE PROS AND CONS OF THE SITUATION. AFTER ALL THE IMAGES HAVE APPEARED, LOOK UP AT THE MOON AND FEEL ITS LIGHT FILL YOU UP, UNTIL YOU ARE BRIMMING WITH THE COOL CLEAR ENERGY OF THE MOON. LOOK AGAIN AT THE POOL AND ASK, "WHAT IS THE BEST OUTCOME?" WATCH AS IMAGES FORM, TELLING YOU WHAT YOU NEED TO KNOW. WHEN YOU UNDERSTAND THE ANSWER, DRINK FROM THE POOL. THANK THE GOD AND GODDESS FOR THEIR ASSISTANCE. RETURN TO YOUR BODY, FOLLOWING YOUR BREATH BACK INTO PHYSICALITY.

YOU ARE REFRESHED AND SERENE.

CREATING CONTINUITY

Permanence, perseverance and persistence in spite of all obstacles, discouragements, and impossibilities: It is this that in all things distinguishes the strong soul from the weak.

—*Thomas Carlyle*

This life is not concerned with health but with healing. This life is not about our being but our becoming. This life is not about rest but about exercise. We are not yet what we shall be, but we are growing toward it. The process is not yet finished but it is going on. This is not the end but it is the road.

—*Martin Luther*

Of all the concerns with a magickal group, continuity is the slipperiest to deal with. As the group moves through stages of development, members will, in general, grow closer together and create deep bonds. Those who do not will usually choose to leave. As your magickal group goes from being new and somewhat disorganized, perhaps with a "we'll make it up as we go along" attitude to a more structured environment people will leave. The natural course of life will take people away. Being an active participant will demand too much time, or too much commitment. If you are a teaching group, you will have members who begin the year as promising, challenging students, but who drop out after a few months because they feel that the work is too hard, or that the class commitment was too much. Cyber groups are even easier to leave than physical ones—it just takes a click of the mouse.

When someone leaves a group, the people remaining may feel shaken, abandoned, or threatened. (They may also feel relieved, even if unable to express it.) If too many people leave a group at once, the group may not survive. Leaving a group makes an implicit statement that the group, or the people in it, isn't valued by the one leaving. Of course, the person who leaves may not mean to make this statement; s/he may have a wide variety of reasons for going. In almost any case, formal leave-taking or a ritual can help the group to recover its integrity. Unfortunately, many people leave groups by simply drifting away, without ever voicing their anger, criticism, or appreciation. If you do value a group, you owe its members (and yourself) a chance to say goodbye.

Over the three years that I was a member of ShadowMoon, we had more than a hundred members, but only half of them actually stayed through their year and a day of training; fewer than that became participants in the core coven. Some left before Dedication, others before Initiation; some left in anger, others because physical life intervened, still others lost interest in the process. Wicca is not a religion for everyone, and many who are attracted to it leave once they realize the depth of commitment required.

ShadowMoon had a particularly interesting problem with continuity. Our High Priestess spent most of a year being seriously ill and unavailable for weeks at a time. Ritual healing helped, but then something else would happen. During the first year, her absences were minimal, and she was able to continue our lessons, more or less on time. The second year was extremely difficult. We created a High Court to provide structure during the High Priestess's increasingly frequent—and long—absences, but the Court did not feel able to act and carry the group forward. We were paralyzed by indecision. The process of transforming our group was painful. It was also burdened by unclear vision: Who were we, and what did we want to do, as individuals and as a group? We had relied entirely on a single person, and without her we felt too fragile to continue. However, as the months went by and we struggled along, we watched members leave, and we learned from our mistakes, pulling the center of the circle in tighter to compensate. Our third year was the smallest in terms of membership, but the most cohesive and creative we had experienced to date, we organically transformed from a triangle into a circle.

Remember that, although you may help someone to step out upon the path of alternative spirituality, s/he will chart her/his own course in the end. Sometimes that means going solitaire, or joining another group. One of the most generous and loving acts a magickal group can perform is to say goodbye to a member who is leaving honorably. In a magickal group, losing a member can truly be likened to losing a member of the family, and other members will experience anger and sadness akin to that felt when someone dies. Depending on the reason for the member's departure, it may be appropriate to hold a ritual of farewell, or perhaps just allow the magickal group to meet and wish them goodbye.

Release of a Magickal Group Member

Preparation:

- ◎ Re-arrange your personal altar, clean it, and spend time with the sacred objects.
- ◎ Choose a memory of a special moment within the group.

~Magickal Connections~

Items needed/Ritual setup:

- ◉ Incense (sandalwood is especially appropriate).
- ◉ A long piece of cord, rope, or other fairly thick piece of string.

Cast the circle and call the Quarters, focusing on:

- ◉ Air's ability to free from attachments.
- ◉ Fire's ability to purify of bonds.
- ◉ Water's ability to wash us clean.
- ◉ Earth's ability to absorb our negativity.

Invoke the Deity.

If the member who left has a sponsor or a special relationship with a current member, that person opens a door in the North, saying:

"In sorrow I say that (<u>full craft name</u>) has chosen to leave (<u>group name</u>). She leaves in silence. She leaves with (no) obligation(s) unfilled."

Each person in the group then speaks about the person starting with *"She leaves…"* (for example: *"She leaves with my friendship."*). It is important to not put anger or negative energy into what you are saying, but to make it a plain statement of fact.

When all have spoken, the ritual leader reaches under the altar and takes out a cord, knotted to the measurements of the departing group member.

The ritual leader says:

"(<u>Craft name</u>), you joined us by crossing a threshold.

Through us you received (<u>degrees, training, or accolades</u>).

You pledged perfect love and perfect trust; you pledged to this Path, you pledged to this group.

~Creating Continuity~

That which has been truly granted by the Gods cannot be taken away but, henceforth, you are known to us only as (<u>mundane name</u>) and are no longer our sister/brother in the Craft.

You have turned from the loving bonds of your spiritual family."

The ritual leader then flicks the cord through the Door to the North, holding one end and watching as the cord unravels completely.

The ritual leader says:

"Thus, we close the door on you—you are released forever. So mote it be!"

The ritual leader turns to face the assembled group and says:

"We stand together, though our circle has been altered.

The sphere, the web, the starlight strands, that sustain our group remain true and strong.

We stand together, reaffirming our loving bonds with one another."

The ritual leader reaches out to take the hand of the person to her/his left, who takes it, the takes that of the person to their left, and so on around the circle until all are joined.

The ritual leader says:

"Feel the strength flowing around our circle endlessly flowing, ever growing."

All breathe and feel bathed in the strength of the energy and say, "Blessed be!"

Bid farewell to the God/dess.

Bid farewell to the Quarters.

Open the Circle.

~Magickal Connections~

Hiving and Other Expansion Issues

There are many things that can be experienced within the safety of the circle or magickal group that a solitary witch can not fully apprehend. One of those things is the process of experiencing grief through the intimate process of hiving off. At its most basic, a hive occurs when the magickal group (either some of its parts or in entirety) chooses to "birth" a new magickal group. There can be several reasons for a hive:

- Sometimes the group will have become too large for the Leaders to administer effectively, so they form smaller groups.

- Perhaps a couple of members will be moving to a new location and wish to found a new (more conveniently located) group.

- It may be that a member finds himself or herself disagreeing with the administration of the group and wishes to do it her (or his) way instead.

- In some cases (mine included), the Deity asks for the event. Although I have known for some time that I should lead a coven, I did not think I was ready. She did. Enough said.

For any reason, in any case, a hive is a serious stressor for the group. A magickal group takes on an identity of its own, made up of the consciousness of each individual member, and when a person leaves it can feel as if a member of your close family has died. One of life's critical transitions for individuals and families is the loss of a loved one. These losses include not only an ending but also a beginning, grief, and mourning. Grieving is a process of discovering what it is that was lost, what is left, and what is possible to do with this hole in your life. Grieving is the transformative process in which loss becomes choices involving growth and finding new stories with new meanings.

~Creating Continuity~

Some people, when they realize a relationship is going to end, will start an argument—that way they avoid the grieving. Righteous anger fuels their departure, soothing their fear, smoothing over their loss. Others withdraw in an attempt to protect themselves from the pain of the loss. So to, when this kind of person feels ties to the group falling apart, he will instigate conflict.

In all types of loss, the severity of the reaction depends upon the degree to which the reality system has been attacked. This reality system is based on personal histories as individuals, families, communities, and society. It dictates how we relate to others in our world. For example, when a parent dies, a large part of the child's reality system is forever changed; what was once safe and nurturing is no longer. Environmental factors also influence such a reaction, including the quality of the relationship before the loss, and the psychological continuity of the individual's surviving environment. Spiritual beliefs, supportive relationships, and positive self-esteem are just a few of the social factors contributing a more balanced recovery of one's world after a severe loss.

Not everyone in the magickal group is going to be at the same place in their grief process. Each member will most likely process various tasks of grief at his own rate and in his own way. Understanding the other members' position and exploring each other's feelings are helpful in restoring the equilibrium to the magickal group. The most potent message from our culture about grief and loss, one of the first we hear and the most often, is not to think about it if at all possible. However, as witches we are *encouraged* to work through our "shadow" emotions, to realize their limited power, and to accept grief as a moment in an endless cycle. How much work do we truly do on this, I wonder? I don't mean that we don't experience grief, loss, depression, or anger, but I question how much time we spend actually exploring these emotions, mapping out the paths they carve within our souls, and just plain thinking about them.

Not allowing ourselves to think about the possible losses in our lives makes a monster out of grief. We do not try it on; we lack flexibility or resourcefulness about it. We keep it buried in our unconscious minds under a heavy topsoil that screams "Danger: Toxic Material!" with an image of a skull and crossbones. This perspective not only inspires a number of unhealthy attitudes towards loss, but also keeps loss associated with death.

Sex, birth, divorce, death, and money have all come out of the closet; these once-taboo topics are now, if not easy, at least accessible topics of conversation. Yet loss and her handmaiden, grief, continue to be taboo, shameful, and hidden.

Our capacity to let go, to lose with grace, awareness, and honor, is supported by having certain developed skills. Each day presents us with the opportunities to hone those skills. I remember when the book *When Bad Things Happen To Good People* came out. My first reaction was: "Define bad things." They are events that happen in life. As a popular bumper sticker puts it: "Compost Happens." (My second reaction was: Who are the "good people" anyway? Who passes that judgment?) How we deal with loss is a manifestation of our relative wellness. Loss happens. Lift the "light" weights of loss that life brings you so that you can see your strengths and weaknesses before the heavier weights pile onto you.

When I sit with someone who asks, "Why me?" I always want to ask in return, "Why not you? Why not now?" Strength comes by practicing with each loss that life brings to us. Daily practice occurs by noticing how we deal with a lost earring, a broken leg, or a broken date. It grows stronger when we examine our fears and resistance as they arise and when we pay attention to the little voices in our minds that say, "I would never be able to deal with _____ ," or "I can not live without _____ ."

~Creating Continuity~

Stop for a moment and ask yourself instead: "What would it take to survive that loss?" Do not diminish your particular struggle with a situation; make no judgments as to your ability or fitness. Use it as a way into your mind and the many thoughts that create your belief systems. How good are you at surrender? At letting go? I am terrible at those skills. Patience is a virtue I desperately need to cultivate. Notice how you respond when plans change. When people change. When the weather gets in your way. When you make a mistake. When you break something. When you are disappointed, or when you disappoint another.

How can we trust our inner wisdom if we have not spent time struggling with it, listening to it, being taught by it? The time to seek our inner teacher is not in the face of disaster; it is in the everyday practice of life and loss. A wise man once said: "While a tree with strong roots can withstand a harsh storm, it can hardly hope to grow them once the storm is on the horizon."[1]

Loss wears many masks. For some of us, the first mask of loss we see is that of betrayal. "This should not happen!" Not only was this loss not in our plans but it happens in a way that is inconceivable to us. Loss comes to us suddenly, unexpectedly, in most cases. But even if we have had time to "prepare" ourselves, as during a lengthy illness or through a drawn-out process of divorce or relocation, we still often find the reality paralyzing. We look for someone to blame: a doctor, a bus driver, a lunatic, the Deity, our spouses, ourselves. Each finger pointing in blame is a pitfall because to place blame means that someone could have done something differently and there would have been a different outcome. Our minds scream, "It wasn't meant to happen this way!"—but who are we to say that?

Remember, again, that we are witches! More so for us than many others, our thoughts not only affect how we feel but also keep us open or closed to the possibilities inherent in any situation. Thoughts are physical energy formed by consciousness. We are more aware than most that "people make their own reality" and therefore are more in control of that process. Our challenge is to be conscious of those thoughts so that we are in charge of them rather than them in charge of us.

Every situation can be compared to an onion skin—with many, many layers—and our task is to stay present as long as it takes to peel away as many of those layers as possible. In this process there's always a teaching. It's rarely the one we thought we signed up for, and seldom one we would have chosen. If we can hold onto the idea that every moment in our lives is potentially teaching us something, and that we always have some choices in the matter, we can hold ourselves open instead of collapsing around our pain, suffering, and sense of betrayal.

Life is unpredictable. There are no guarantees of what will happen next. The Tibetans say: "Tomorrow or the next life, which comes first we cannot know." That very unpredictability holds loss at its center. What we need and have today might no longer be ours tomorrow. This gives rise to the question of whether it was "ours" from the beginning. Trust in the ebb and flow of life is essential to our well-being: We trust that the tides will rise and fall, the sun will come up each morning, and the seasons will follow each other. Can we trust that there is meaning and wisdom in the gifts and losses of our lives? More importantly, can we include betrayal—which is another kind of loss—in that trust?

It is important for the group to work, actively, to integrate and resolve our grief, not to just passively experience our reactions. Grief carries us until we learn to carry it. It seems to me that there are certain tasks to perform when grieving. They are:

- ◉ To express all the feelings over this loss: anguish, longing, relief, anger, depression, numbness, despair, aching, guilt, confusion, and pain.

~Creating Continuity~

◉ To review your relationships from the beginning and to see the positive and negative aspects.

◉ To identify and heal your unresolved issues and your regrets.

◉ To explore the changes within your magickal group and other relationships.

◉ To integrate all the changes into a new sense of yourself and to take on healthy new ways of being in the world without this person, this group.

◉ To form a healthy new inner relationship and to find new ways of relating to people.

Perhaps that sounds as if it's a great deal of work to do for a person who has only left the group, rather than the world. A hiving, however, offers a special opportunity to explore many aspects of loss and grief in a safe, nurturing environment. It is a changing experience, not just in terms of who does what, but also in terms of the Group mind's "feel" and its quality of energy. A hive affects the magickal group on many levels: physically, astrally, and etherically. To ignore the opportunity to explore those changes is a loss of another nature.

In the end, what I understand is this: Grieving is the process of moving into the emotional and spiritual realms that the months and years ahead offer to us. It is a journey, not a destination. We all grieve because we have loved, and through our journey we can be healed.

Despite the sadness, the birth of a daughter magickal group, similar to the creation of the beehive from which the term 'hiving' is taken, is a vital task of a magickal group's growth and continuity. Hiving is not necessary, but to be large enough, or have trained members enough that you feel it is time to create a new magickal group in your lineage, is a proud moment for your magickal group. Celebrate the birth! There is a sharp pain of loss as the "daughter" or "son" leaves the magickal group, but also of joy at his or her accomplishments; reframe your grief into the satisfaction of a job well done. Mark the occasion with a special magickal group blessing, a ritual that empowers her/him to lead well and wisely, and offers a sense of closure for the community s/he leaves behind.

My own hiving came with being raised to the Third Degree. As I stood in the sacred space, looking at my High Priestess and High Priest, feeling the God/dess energy completely suffusing me, I underwent a dramatic internal transformation. The Lisa who emerged from that ritual is not the woman who went into it. It is a bittersweet memory, if only for the loss that accompanies such a transition, but a cherished one. When my own coven birthed a daughter this year, it was not as profound a change for me personally, but JaguarMoon has altered and the dynamics have transformed into something none of us expected. The mother coven is now quite small (only four members) but stronger for the process. Just as a rose bush is after a good pruning, it is small and cut back, but able to grow stronger, healthier branches to create superb blooms.

A healthy, living magickal group or Tradition needs a combination of continuity and change. Ideally these elements exist in balance or in a flowing cycle, because continuity without change is stagnant, and change without continuity is chaotic.

GROUPS—PAGAN OR NOT—TEND TO FOLLOW A CYCLE THAT IS NOT UNLIKE THAT OF A TREE GROWING. THERE IS THE INITIAL STAGE OF FERTILIZATION, WHEN THE SEED BEGINS TO SPROUT. ROOTS REACH DEEP INTO THE EARTH TO GET VITAL NUTRIENTS. IN A GROUP, THIS STAGE IS ONE OF EXPLORATION: EVERYTHING AND EVERYONE IS NEW AND SHINY. DURING THIS TIME, WE TEND TO TRY TO BE ON OUR "BEST BEHAVIOR" SO THAT EVERYONE WILL LIKE US. OUR SEED BREAKS THE SURFACE AND, IF PROPERLY WARMED BY THE SUN AND WATERED BY THE RAIN, IT GROWS STRONG AND QUICKLY. IN THE GROUP, THIS STAGE CORRESPONDS TO ONE IN WHICH MEMBERS FEEL COMFORTABLE ENOUGH TO SHOW SOME

~Creating Continuity~

PARTS OF THEIR "NOT PERFECT" PERSONALITIES. A CAREFUL GROUP LEADER WILL NURTURE THE GROUP THROUGH THIS TIME OF STRENGTHENING TIES AND DEEPENING TRUST.

BUT, AS THE SPROUT BECOMES A SAPLING, OUTSIDE FORCES HAVE A GREATER IMPACT ON IT. BECAUSE IT DOES NOT YET HAVE THE DEEP, FIRMLY SEATED ROOTS TO HOLD IT FAST WHEN HIGH WINDS BLOW, OR TO NOURISH IT WITH WATER UNDERGROUND IN TIMES OF DROUGHT, IT CAN BE DAMAGED. FOR MANY GROUPS, THIS STAGE IS THE "MAKE IT OR BREAK IT" TIME. THE GROUP QUESTIONS ITS OWN IDENTITY, DEMANDING NEW WAYS OF DEALING WITH OLD ISSUES. FACTIONS FORM AND DISSOLVE. IT IS AS IF EVERYTHING IS CHANGING ALL THE TIME, AND THE GROUP IS IN CHAOS.

IF THE SAPLING SURVIVES THE VAGARIES OF THE OUTSIDE WORLD, HOWEVER, IT BECOMES ITS DESTINY: A TREE. DEEPLY ROOTED WITHIN THE EARTH, BRANCHES RAISED HIGH TO CATCH THE WARMTH OF THE SUN, DRINKING THE RAIN AND MOVING WITH THE WIND. GROUPS THAT MAKE IT TO THIS STAGE CAN FEEL VERY PROUD OF THEMSELVES AS A STRONG SENSE OF IDENTITY AND COHESION FORMS.

UNLIKE A TREE, HOWEVER, HUMAN INTERACTION FLOWS IN CYCLES. THEREFORE, IF YOUR GROUP IS SUCCESSFUL, YOU WILL FIND YOURSELF GOING THROUGH THESE STAGES OVER AND OVER AGAIN, EACH TIME IN A SLIGHTLY DIFFERENT MANNER. IT IS OKAY—IN FACT, IT IS GREAT.

After the 1st Year: Special Issues

This discussion is for when you have made it through your first year together. For some groups, it may take longer to get to this point, and for others it may come very quickly. You are getting ready to go beyond anything I can tell you to do. Different groups will have different needs at an advanced level; each is unique, and the problems you will handle, the people you have asked to join you are particular to your vision; I cannot see for you. However, I can take you through some ideas for creating your future, once you move past the initial stages.

~Magickal Connections~

Ritual-Based Group

Keep *doing* ritual, any kind of ritual, whether for spell work, moon magick, or meditative journeys. As you do ritual, you will get more comfortable in the doing. But—and there is always a "but"—be very clear about the ground rules. This is not a problem if you are in a hierarchical group, where things are fairly well structured, but, if you belong to a freeform gathering or circle, ritual can get chaotic, quickly. I strongly recommend that you have a leader for each ritual. Even if it is a rotating leadership, or the roles are performed by a number of people, or whatever the variation is, you need a single person to give direction to the ritual.

If in doubt as to whether it will work, try it anyway. And if it does not work the first time, go back and tinker with it until it does. The God/dess loves laughter; being able to laugh at your own follies is an important part of being human.

Information Sharing Group

Groups that meet to share information benefit from being large; the more points of view, the more experiences, the less likely it is that you will run out of things to share. On the other hand, you will probably find that the same questions arise, in a somewhat predictable way. (The repeating cycle of answering these questions is what led Lady Mystara to found ShadowMoon.) They are not bad questions, and they are very important to know the answer to these questions when you are new to the Craft. But it is difficult to remain upbeat and positive when you are answering them for the 4,173rd time.

If your group seems to be losing a little steam and the activity is dropping down, try using one of the following topics to wake it up again. There is no such thing as a bad topic, but there are superficial topics—which are just reasons to chat. Social conversation is great, but it will not sustain a group for a long period of time.

When you propose a topic, it is a good idea to give it some help. Find a short—or long!—reading to open the discussion or provide some background. It is important to make sure that no one opinion is the "right" one, and that many sides of the issue are explored. Some topics turn out to be extremely sensitive (for example, economic status and racial issues). If you suspect that might be the case, opening the discussion with a gentle reminder that what is shared within the group is confidential and acknowledging the tenderness of the subject can help create a feeling of safety among participants.

Here are some interesting topics for discussion:

- Where do you first turn in a crisis? Does it vary by the situation, or do you tend to respond the same way, time after time?

- How were religion and spirituality seen and treated in your childhood home? What is the faith of your families?

- How are you teaching your children about faith and/or religion? What sources do you use? Do you do rituals with them?

- How do you perceive yourself within nature? What fears do you have about the outdoors? What keeps you inside? How do you connect with nature?

- What memories do you have of being artistic as a child? How did they affect you as an adult? What obstacles are there to your being creative? What artistic activities bring you pleasure? Are you a perfectionist? What atmosphere is conducive to your creativity?

- What have you learned from our ancestors? Who were they? Where did they come from? What stories can we tell of them?

- Who are your role models? Why? Were any of them related to you?

- What is your relationship with food? Is it your friend or enemy? Do you use or abuse food? How was food treated while you were a child? How does food bring you pleasure? Pain? Do you cook? How is food connected to your spirituality?

- Do you consider yourself beautiful? How has your definition of beauty changed? How do beauty and spirituality relate with one another? When are you the most beautiful? The ugliest?

- What do you think of when you consider power? Do you think of yourself as powerful? Describe power and how you wield it, and when. Who is the most powerful person you know? Are there different kinds of power? How do you sabotage your own power?

- What does money mean? What was your family's economic status growing up? How has that changed? What is "enough" money? How does money move through your life? Are you financially "healthy"? What does that mean to you?

- What has been your experience with death? What do you think dying is like? What makes you afraid about death? Do you think about death? What do you think happens?

Considerations for Younger Witches

A magickal group created by and for young people will be very different than one for adults only. Many magickal groups

~Creating Continuity~

will not accept teenagers because they are wary of state laws regarding influencing a minor. It can be disheartening to feel the call of the Lord and Lady and yet be denied learning because of the fleeting status of age. Teen cyber magickal groups provide support and learning during this time, and there are many such groups. Unfortunately many do not last more than a year.

If you cannot find a group you feel comfortable with or live in an environment that does not encourage spiritual exploration, then I encourage you to wait. As hard as that is to do, a solitary working can be a test of one's dedication to a chosen path. To wait, however, does not mean that you cannot prepare or deepen your knowledge and understanding of the Mysteries. Here are some specific suggestions about how to prepare for formal Craft training:

1. **School and Study.** As long as you are in school, it will pay off for you to become the best possible student. In modern witchcraft, there are few paid clergy. Preparing for a good job with adequate monetary compensation is a way of ensuring that you are supported by a livelihood you enjoy. Research a variety of career paths. The research, organizational skills, and habits of concentration that develop also will be useful for Craft study and work. As well, being able to support yourself gives you a great deal of strength, power, and self-confidence—all marks of a great witch!

2. **Read.** If you can safely obtain and read such basic primers as Starhawk's *Spiral Dance*, Margot Adler's *Drawing Down the Moon*, any of the numerous Farrar books, then do so. You may wish to seek out deeper meanings within your families' religion. There are many valuable lessons found within different religious systems, not just Paganism. The Craft is a difficult Path to follow and, if you do not have to leave the religion of your birth, perhaps you should not.

~Magickal Connections~

I encourage you to learn about the many sister paths of Paganism as well. Do some thorough research on the history, mythos, and practices of different ethnic cultures. Visit museums to see the relics from those cultures, and listen to relevant music from days gone by (Celtic pieces, bardic folk songs, and so on). Take every opportunity to experience Pagan cultures; seek them out. This study should take you into accessible and relevant anthropological, historical, theological, and psychological works rather than the specific occult books, which can limit your perspective.

3. **Meditation.** This is the single most important skill you can learn and practice. It should be a daily exercise, giving you the benefits of concentration and serenity. Meditation will also help you understand your studies and/or develop all of your talents. It will also help you to exercise the willed imagination, which is basic to Wiccan ritual work. It requires no props or tools that may give you away to suspicious or snoopy parents. If there is little peace at home, you can meditate in a quiet corner of the library!

Keep a personal journal that covers your reading, meditation experience, dreams, and anything else of interest. The basic theme of the journal should be: "What does all of this mean for me?" Writing things down will help you to notice and understand how different ideas and experiences are related, both to each other and to your personal needs and growth. Should your parents have no respect for their privacy, you may want to leave the journal in a locker at school, or another secure place.

4. **Artistic Expression.** I strongly encourage you to work hard at developing your own particular art or talent. Artistic expression will help you open channels of the creative

and imaginative self within, which is the first and easiest way to encounter the Gods that live in and through us. Many Pagans use their artistic skills for tool-making or ritual performance.

5. Nature. Our Mysteries are about the sacredness of life here on Earth, right now. We are "nature worshipers," so nature is a sacred duty. Watch the moon wax and wane, plant a garden of herbs of flowers, and attune to the cycles of our Mother. Volunteer for a community project to clean up an environmentally affected area. I invite you to spend as much time as possible outside and off the pavements, and to keep your heart open and senses alert.

Please note that none of these suggestions call for activities that would raise suspicion with parental units. Nor will following any of these ideas do you harm to you in any way, but they will help you feel more grounded and connected. Having a focused mind, a means of creative expression, a job that is fulfilling, and a greater understanding of nature will improve you, regardless of where you use them! Above all, you will know what it is like to pursue a goal independently, becoming a more self-directed and balanced adult.

A note of caution: There is no "patent" on the word *witch*, and there are many out there who claim to be competent and ethical, but in no way adhere to either of those attributes. The group may be sexually dysfunctional or use drugs or alcohol irresponsibly, to their advantage. Some live up to the image of a "cult" using mind control and exploitation, or use baneful magicks, causing inevitable psychological and karmic rebounds.

If you really want to work with others, I have an alternative: Form a study-group.

~Magickal Connections~

You will still have to work hard and be honest with your-self, but most of the negative side effects can be avoided. In addition to the books I mentioned earlier, here is a list of books to start with:[3]

- *Wicca: A Guide For The Solitary Practitioner* by Scott Cunningham.
- *To Ride A Silver Broomstick* by Silver RavenWolf.
- *Raising Witches: Teaching the Wiccan Faith to Children* by Ashleen O'Gaea.
- *Calling The Circle* by Christina Baldwin.

Each book has a bibliography, so use them to choose your next readings. Enjoy your travels!

When the study-group has devoured a few books, with each individual also branching out to read more, start talking about what you read. Discuss what made sense, or did not. Talk about your impressions, thoughts, feelings, likes, and dislikes. Strive to understand all you can read. If you are doing well, someone will want to join your study group. Allow the newcomer to pick a member of the study group to be a mentor. It would be good to only have those who feel confident in their teaching abilities act as mentors. You may wish to think about creating a reading list for newcomers and guidelines for discussion.

If your group has an adult advisor, it may be a very good idea if everyone agrees to the "rules" of their involvement. To the adult, I say:

1. Do not try to "lead"; your job is to advise and support. Teens learn leadership and independence only through practice as leaders and as independent members. Allow as much freedom in self-direction as possible and serve as a

teacher and friend. Instead of dictating, provide information and let the teens stay in control.

2. Avoid personal involvement. An advisor who maintains total objectivity will be trusted and listened to. A teen group should be a peer-directed group that has the support of a "wise" adult who is always available but never intrusive.

These next two are so obvious they need not be said, but just in case...

3. Absolutely no sexual involvement or flirtatious dialogue is appropriate. Aside from the legal prohibition, the ethic commonly called "the Rede" requires that we harm none, and the potential for harm when an older person is romantically involved with a younger one is always present. Violating this law can be costly not only to the advisor, but also to the group and to the Craft as a whole.

4. Do not provide or condone the use of drugs. Again, this is a legal issue. "Contributing to the delinquency of a minor" is a serious charge, and with laws, an advisor who allows teen drug use in her/his home or car faces severe penalties if discovered. There is also the consideration that there is convincing evidence that the use of drugs, even marijuana, by adolescents can disrupt the emotional maturation process.

Lesson Plans—Beginning and Intermediate

If you have created a teaching magickal group it is likely that you spent a great deal of time formulating a group of lessons to teach. The learning one receives in magickal arts is frequently only the beginning of what we then spend our entire lives mastering. To do a detailed lesson plan would require more room than this book allows for, but here is the outline of studies taught by JaguarMoon: (Two others are found in Appendix G and H.)

Basic Intro to Wicca (August–September): Magickal group structure, general terms, the Rede and magickal ethics, magickal group laws, Craft and magick, choosing a Craft name, numerology, creating a BoS, ritual tools, creating an altar/sacred space, basic meditation, creating a moon diary, creating a dream diary.

Understanding the Faces of the Deity (September): The Crone and the Sage.

The Art of Ritual (October–November): Sabbats versus Esbats, circle casting, quarter calls, invocations, components of ritual, ethics of ritual creation, moon rituals, Sabbat rituals, Rites of Passage, bathing, colors, candles, incense, oils.

Divination (December–January): Basic astrology, introduction to runes, stones, tarot, dream work.

Understanding the Faces of the Deity (December): The Hidden Faces: the Warrior and the Dark God/dess.

History of Wicca (February): History of Goddess Worship, pre- and post-Gardnerian Wicca, the "Old" Religion and the Craft today.

Advanced Mental Work (March): Meditation, relaxation, focus, projection, and visualization.

Understanding the Faces of the Deity (March): The Maiden and the Youth.

The Spirit World (April): The spirit world, spirit guides, totems.

Basic Healing Work (May): Terms and techniques—an overview, basic herbal medicine, distance healing, chakra work, ethics of magickal healing.

Moving On (June): Magickal paths and traditions, Initiation, and degrees.

Understanding the Faces of the Deity (June): The Mother and the Lover.

Initiation, Degrees, and the Evolution of the Self

The majority of my training has focused on Wicca, the oldest "new" religion in existence. As with many Pagan belief systems, Wicca's roots lie in pre-historical cultures, greatly modified by modern reality. A crucial difference between Wicca and other Pagan religions (including the larger group of Witchcraft is that we are an initiatory mystery religion. When I speak of Initiation it is from my perspective as a Witch, and a Wiccan. I have not undergone Initiation in any other religion, and so I cannot speak to its viewpoint.

Wicca has little dogma, and so our truth lies within two realms: metaphysical and psychological. Our belief system is founded upon the simple knowledge that our consciousness is not dependent upon the physical senses, but allows for the existence of an unseen realm, accessible through our psychic senses. As well, we believe in the reverence of the life force within us all, and found in the worlds surrounding us. Because of this reverence for the life force, the Divinity within us all, we believe that we all have the power and authority of free will. Free will can be clearly seen in the conscious choices made, but it is also apparent in the unconscious decisions that are more difficult to discern. As our understanding of our history has evolved, so has our conception of the changes that we undergo through the process of initiation and the transformation of the Self. As we walk the path of Initiation, we can look back and see, with increasing clarity, how our journey has changed us, and how we in turn have changed the path. This does not mean that we wake up one day and realize that we have all the answers, but instead that we begin to un- derstand how much we have yet to learn, and why it is that our knowledge must grow over lifetimes, instead of mere years.

Contrary to some things I have read, being a Witch is not as simple as saying "I am a Witch" aloud three times. It is an ongoing process of deepening understanding of your Self and the Divinity within. For many people, the first Initiation also acts as an acknowledgment that an interaction between the Divine and the Self has occurred, and the individual is aware of his or her own Divinity. My first Initiation in 1981 was a simple ceremony I created with a bit of salt, a candle, a stick of incense, and a cup of water. Although I have had several Initiations since then, that memory of opening myself up and seeing the potential I held within myself will never leave me. Reading is not enough, although it can provide an excellent introduction.

Practicing magick creates psychological and psychic changes within you. Seeing those changes is one thing; accept- ing them is another. Most of the work of magick is in the acceptance and awareness of those unconscious motivations. Simply put, your magick will not succeed if you or any part of you does not wish it to, or if the beneficiary of your magick refuses the assistance. To minimize this conflict, we engage in focus, visualization, and meditation exercises. We also ask for Divine assistance in making the "correct" choices, rather than blindly choosing an option.

A magickal group has a difficult task to accomplish with every ritual: It must take a group of individual consciousnesses and meld them into what is generally called a "Group mind."

~Creating Continuity~

This primarily involves trust on the part of the individuals, because the process is one in which the barriers between each psyche must be opened and a portion of the consciousness melded with all of the other portions. This creates a new entity entirely, one without a directive consciousness, but powerful nonetheless. It's as if you each donate a piece of masonry, with which a strong wall is built.

The creation of a magickal group of any nature will also create a Group mind, but without a formal acknowledgment, it will not be particularly strong or stable. The longer a group is in existence, the stronger the Group mind will become. Resembling a tree, the leaders twine around one another, forming the trunk, and directly connected to the other members who are connected via branches to one another. The Group mind is built out of love, trust, and acceptance. If a magickal group is formed and Dedicated in a ceremony, the Group mind is made stronger, and each successive ritual only strengthens the ties between the members.

The process of an Initiation into a magickal group opens the "circle" of the Group mind and accepts the new member into the group. It allows the new person to access the energy of the Group mind, as well as to experience the closeness of the group as a whole. It creates a feeling of kinship, of family. It is as if you are invited into the storeroom of the magickal group's spiritual energy, free to both increase and use it when necessary. This ritual opens the mind to the expansion of consciousness that accompanies the linkage into the Group mind, but it does not actually bestow any new powers or insights upon you. You are shown the door, and the Initiation opens the gate in that doorway.

If you belong to a hierarchical group, you will generally have several more degrees available to you. But moving beyond the First Degree is:

a) Not required, and

b) Not necessary.

I cannot emphasize that enough.

A Second Degree Initiation is a huge responsibility. You are, in effect, accepting karmic ties to myour intiator, the magickal group, as well as each person you teach and initiate thereafter. At the same time, you are telling the God and Goddess that you think you are ready to be their Priest/ess throughout your lifetimes—and they will test your resolve. Sounds a bit ominous? It should. Many people, when they feel they are ready to take their Second, suddenly have their lives change in sad, awful, difficult ways. They lose their job, their lover leaves, or someone close to them dies. Their life is turned upside down—they live the Tarot's Tower card to its fullest meanings. The message of that card is "spiritual purification." The Divine fire scorches you and leaves you transformed, melted, and you re-form into a purer aspect. Do I make it sound pretty? It is not.

In the end, you are clear in all aspects of your Self as to why you are a Second Degree and that you wish to guide others on the path of Wicca. At the least, you are competent to create and lead rituals, you understand the elemental forces you are summoning and manipulating, and you can handle odd disruptions within the circle. As well, you are making a contribution to your community—either the witch community or that of your mundane life. This contribution may be in any form you feel is appropriate and becomes clear to you during the "transformation" time you experience. In some traditions, you are considered to be qualified to lead a magickal group at this point, and so would "hive off" to form a daughter magickal group within your Tradition.

Most people never take their Second Degree, because they understand themselves well enough to realize that it is not a promotion, or similar to getting a master's degree on a career path. It is an obligation and a karmic agreement that you make that will follow you through many lifetimes. It is a permanent commitment to the priesthood and to the services of the God/dess.

The Third Degree Initiation occurs when the Witch feels s/he is ready to be a leader of a magickal group, and has acquired all the skills necessary to do so. Again, this Degree is NOT a promotion, but more of an acknowledgment of a particular skill set that has been achieved. One of my favorite descriptions of what is required to be a Third Degree is along the lines of "you'll know when you're ready." It's a bit simplistic, but nonetheless true. The God/dess will tell you when you are ready for your Third Degree, and the transformation will frequently happen outside of any magickal group ritual. (This ritual is usually a confirmation rather than a trigger.)

If I meet a person who is quick to give me her "I'm a 3rd Degree WitchQueen" speech, I generally assume she is exaggerating, if not actually lying, about her qualifications. Your initiatory degree is not an award given for good service, or a means to convince people to follow you. The quiet people in the corner, watching the crowd and sipping a latte, are more likely to be the WitchQueens, and I will head toward their quiet air of acceptance, and authority, every time.

The Third Degree indicates an awareness that the Self has transformed and a feeling of total acceptance is operating. Generally Thirds are tranquil and serene—not always, but strife passes quickly and causes less disturbance. There is a feeling of balance, that the anima/animus, male/female, yin/yang aspects are in harmony, understood for their positive and negative aspects. This person has given up her own needs to serve the needs of others and is comfortable in that role. Although the process was begun in the Second Degree, it is expressed more clearly in this stage.

~Magickal Connections~

As you can see, the primary teaching of Wicca is the transformation of the Self. All of this knowledge may be acquired without external validation (that is, Degrees), but they do provide a "signpost" as to where you are along the journey. I recently had a class member come to me about a series of dreams she had been having over a couple of weeks. Thematically they were very similar: She traveled through a forested landscape and came upon a huge, gorgeous Goddess who enfolded her into Herself and birthed her anew. "Is this," she wrote, "an Initiation?" My reply was to ask her if she felt different, was a different person, than before the dreams.

Initiation is a verb, not a noun; a process, not a title.

To change one's life:
Start immediately
Do it flamboyantly
No exceptions.
—William James

ART OF RITUAL CLASS APPLICATION

This application is the one used in the groups I have worked with since 1997. It provides an example of one way of screening potential group members and can be modified to meet your group's needs.

Please answer each question to the best of your ability. Remember that the more we know about you, the better we can determine whether our class will meet your needs, desires, and expectations.

I. Spirituality and Self-Knowledge

1. How do you define your religion/spirituality?
2. What led you to your religion?
3. What are your strengths?
4. What are your weak points?
5. What previous training degrees have you received? Was it with a group, personal teacher, self-taught?

~Magickal Connections~

If you worked with others previously:

- ◉ Tell us more about the training and experience with these groups.
- ◉ What did you like about working with others?
- ◉ What did not you like?

6. Have you ever trained another person in the Craft? If yes:

- ◉ Describe that experience.
- ◉ Are you still in contact with that person (those people) now?
- ◉ What (How) are they doing?

II. Daily Life

1. Do you have a partner? What is your relationship?
2. Do you have children?
3. Does your immediate family share your religious beliefs? If not, what are their beliefs?
4. How do they feel about your being a witch?
5. Are you "in" or "out" regarding your religious beliefs? To what degree?
6. Do you have any work/life conflicts that will prevent you from attending online rituals and/or meetings?
7. Do you have any physical conditions that could interfere with your ability to attend online rituals and/or meetings?

III. Class Specific

1. What calls you to learn this information?
2. What do you expect from the class?

3. What do you expect from the group?

4. Where did you hear about us?

5. How would you rate your technical knowledge and computer experience?

6. What kind of computer and operating system do you use?

IV. Basic Information (***This information will not be revealed in any fashion outside of the decision-making group.***)

1. What is your name (Craft and mundane)?

2. What is your mailing address?

3. What is your phone number?

4. What is your date of birth?

5. What is your preferred e-mail address?

6. Do you have any Web pages?

Is there anything else you think we should know about you?

The deadline to return the application is midnight (Pacific Time), May 30th.

ART OF RITUAL CLASS AGREEMENT

This agreement is given to class members at the start of the year. It provides a context for the new students to understand, succinctly, the teachers' perspective about the various backgrounds, beliefs, and training usually found among class members.

1. An It Harm None, Do What Ye Will.

This can be reworded like this: "If there is absolutely no harm done by your actions or in-actions insofar as you and those you are close to or Working with can possibly imagine, then go ahead and do or not do it. If there is ANY chance of harm being done by your actions or in-action, don't. This is the core of our ethical system. It applies to your daily life just as much as to any magickal work."

2. Self-Initiation Is Perfectly Valid.

You do not need to be initiated by anyone to make your Path a valid one...but admit to the fact that you are self-initiated, and don't make up an impressive "genealogy," for you will only be fooling yourself. If you are self-initiated, be proud of it. You are just as "initiated" as the person who can trace their line back (supposedly) to the Burning Times or to Gerald Gardner.

3. A Solitary Witch Is Still A Witch.

You do not have to belong to a Coven, Circle or any group to be a Witch, though it is a good idea to meet with and network with others, both for the fellowship, and to learn more.

4. Read! Read! Read.

a. Read everything you can lay your hands on about Craft and Magick. Read both pro and con about it (we try to present balanced Point of Views in the class, but its not always possible).

b. Think about what you have read, don't just accept it as true until you have verified its worth to you.

5. There Is No "One True Tradition" Of Wicca.

"If it works, it's real." This applies to ritual, names of the Deity(s), the clothing that you wear (or don't wear), everything. If it works for you, it's real. If it doesn't work, then it's not real. It's as simple as that!

6. Other Belief Systems Are Valid Paths.

We should not denigrate these beliefs simply because of the perversions of their otherwise good and useful teachings by people who had/have a political/religious/social axe to grind. We can learn much from the Bible, the Torah, and the Koran. Their ethical and moral systems have been proven to work.

7. Any Action That Is Illegal By Secular Law Is Illegal Within Craft.

This one is self-explanatory, folks, and does not cover such laws as might forbid co-habitation, multiple significant others,

~Appendix B~

or homosexuals, but it does apply to such things as will harm another, or bring the Craft into disrepute. Things like drugs, sexual relations with minors, animal sacrifice, vandalism, being a public nuisance, and the like are illegal.

8. Many Traditions, One God/dess.

a. There are many, many forms of Wicca. Some of these may not be right for you. Keep looking until you find one that is.

b. Don't be afraid to say "no!" if you feel something is being asked of you that you cannot accept.

c. Don't be afraid to walk out of the group if you don't like what's going on. Think for yourself!

9. Participate In The Class Daily.

This doesn't mean posting daily, necessarily, but making time, every day, to do class work. Otherwise you'll be rushing through on weekends and you will not get as much out of the learning as a result. (I speak from personal experience.)

10. Speak Out, Speak Politely.

Online communication is text-based and reactive. Keep that in mind if you are feeling like no one is paying attention to you or your needs. Do we *know* you need something? (How do we know, did you tell us?) "Speak politely" is a reminder that we are equals here and disrespect or rudeness is not how we treat each other.

11. We Are All Valuable.

We all have information to share. You do not have to accept another's judgment of you as correct.

12. We Are In Service To The Lord And Lady.

In the end, it for our betterment and Their glory.

~Magickal Connections~

Lady Maat's Responsibilities

This document is given to the class along with the Agreement. It arose from a realization that expectations are (ideally) an equal responsibility between teacher and student. (Lady Maat is the author's Craft name.)

1. To train and nurture *your* personal abilities and capacities—not as a reflection of my own image, but as true vision of you.

2. To listen to you, with an open mind and loving heart, *especially* when you are criticizing me.

3. To be accountable for all decisions I make.

4. To support your power to disagree with me.

5. To maintain clear lines of authority within the group, revealing hidden agendas and denying covert power plays.

6. To keep any commitments I make to you.

7. To delegate tasks as needed.

8. To train others to take my place.

9. To not deny my personal needs, or ask that you deny yours.

10. To practice politeness, exercise common courtesy and act with respect, always.

11. To create a safe environment for the expression of feelings, while defining boundaries to protect participants.

12. To admit my mistakes and correct them.

JaguarMoon Compact

A compact is a document that simply and clearly states the "ground rules" of a coven's philosophy and procedures. The following is my coven's.

Statement of Purpose

JaguarMoon is a cyber coven in the American Eclectic Wiccan Tradition, descended from ShadowMoon cyber coven (now defunct). Our primary focus is to teach the religion of Wicca on the Internet. Our secondary goal is to worship the Lord and Lady. Thirdly, we work together as a coven, doing magick, creating community, and sharing knowledge. Our first and most important Law is: *An it Harm None, Do What ye Will.*

Our Tradition

We are an entirely virtual teaching Tradition following the path of American Eclectic Wicca (AEW). AEW is sometimes used to refer to a broad range of individuals or groups that base their philosophy, rituals, and practices on the published works of modern American Witches like Scott Cunningham and Starhawk. American Eclectics frequently take the position that Wicca is a completely modern religion created by Gerald Gardner but that the beliefs and practices of Wicca are rooted within historical teachings. In general, American Eclectics emphasize spontaneity and a strong sense of "use what works, discard what doesn't."

In JaguarMoon we believe that Oaths, Lineage, Initiations, and Traditions are very important for the strength of the connections we form with one another. We may not be lineaged in a traditional manner, but we intend to go forward creating our own branching Tradition. To that end, we prefer structure to chaos, writing down what works and using it again, making changes as needed (preferably by consensus), and a preference for keeping an eye on what we will evolve into rather than making it up as we go along.

Our coven is a wheel, which morphs in and out of a snowflake shape with the inclusion of the students. At the center is the High Priestess, the coven members are linked directly to her, and with one another; students are linked to their mentor and (loosely) to one another.

Basic Operating Rules

JaguarMoon has several rules that are vital to the coven's strength.

I. Respect

We will always respect one another's opinions, beliefs, and attitudes. Disagreement is tolerated, questioning is encouraged, but it must be done in a courteous manner. We understand and live in accordance with the knowledge that almost nothing is absolutely certain, and the other person is as correct in their perception as we are. If misunderstandings occur, members are asked to try and "see the other side." Our coven is a practice of discernment, not judgment—someone else's view is not right or wrong, only different.

2. Honesty

Honesty is required. This includes the honesty of self-awareness and the ability to say no when appropriate. In a cyber coven, much more so than in a physical group, it is difficult for others to discern your true needs. Speaking up for your self is true honesty.

3. Privacy

All information shared within the coven is private and treated as confidential. What we share with one another is not to be shown to anyone outside the coven (although permission may be granted by the creator to copy the information, or to give it to an outsider). All information regarding coven members' physical names, addresses, telephone numbers, etc. is NOT to be revealed to ANY non-coven member.

Violations of privacy are not tolerated and the responsible party will be dismissed from the coven.

4. You Are Responsible

Online communication lacks many of the informative nuances of physical meetings. You are the only one who can speak up for yourself, no one else will notice if you are sad, or quiet, or having a bad day. If you need something, anything, you must ask for it. We will give it to you as best we can, but you must ask. If you do not like how a situation is handled, it is your responsibility to communicate that feeling. As well, if you are asked to do something and you cannot, then speak up and say no. Personal responsibility is the heart of being a witch and the coven is an ideal place to explore your boundaries and strengths as you accept and refuse responsibilities.

~Magickal Connections~

5. Ritual Attendance

All rituals—Sabbat and Esbat—are to be attended by every member of the coven. We recognize that Life and the (sometimes) delicate nature of Internet communication can prevent a member from joining a ritual. However, we expect that every attempt will be made to attend, or that apologies will be made prior to the ritual—either to the Coven Coordinator, the High Priestess, or one's mentor.

Logs of our rituals can be made by any member of the coven, but are not to be shared with non-coven people, or with members of the coven who did not attend the ritual. If a coven member wishes to receive ritual outline it may be available. The High Priestess will make that decision, and the ritual itself can be obtained from the Coven Coordinator.

Coven Laws

The Laws of this coven are divided into three areas: Mundane, Physical and Spiritual. The Mundane Laws (also known as the Coven By-Laws) are to be published and available to any person who makes a request. The Physical and Spiritual Laws are private and shared only amongst coven members. Exceptions can be made, with the consensus agreement of the Council of Elders.

Compact Review

This Compact is an agreement amongst all coven members. It is also a document that is not "set in stone" for as the world changes, so should our selves within it. Each year, near the start of the year (between Litha and Mabon) this document shall be reviewed and discussed by all coven members. Any changes will be made at that time, and the document signed anew.

~Appendix C~

This Compact is an agreement amongst all coven members. It is also a document that is not "set in stone" for as the world changes, so should our selves within it. Therefore we shall strive to review and discuss this document each year, near the start of the year (between Litha and Mabon). Any changes will be made at that time, and the document signed anew.

All Hail JaguarMoon!
Created by Lady Maat, High Priestess
Approved by the Council of Elders

JAGUARMOON DEDICANT AGREEMENT

Those wishing to join JaguarMoon must go through the Art of Ritual class, thus giving us a year to get to know them, and for them to decide that our is the Path they wish to continue on. When they join as a Dedicant, they are given the following documents.

Those who wish to join JaguarMoon must:

1. Have a strong desire to explore Wicca as a potential personal spiritual path, and this coven as a potential spiritual family;

2. Agree that neither the identities of the members, nor any coven business, nor any member's personal business, shall be shared outside the group without the express permission of those involved;

3. Have lives that are settled enough to have room, physically and emotionally, for powerful new experiences and personal growth;

4. Have the support of significant others in the decision to become a Dedicant;

5. Have schedules which allow participation in most coven activities (classes, esbats, sabbats, etc.);

6. Agree to use all knowledge shared by the teachers in the spirit of the Wiccan Rede;

7. Make a serious, good-faith effort to get to know all the other coven members and build good relationships with them;

8. Begin to create or obtain basic ritual tools (athame, wand or staff, chalice, pentacle, candlesticks, salt and water bowls) and set up a personal altar at home;

9. Agree to abide by the attendance requirements and by-laws of this coven; and

10. Understand that participation as a Dedicant does not guarantee eventual initiation into the Craft or the coven.

~Appendix D~

If the above rules seem reasonable to you, then you will be asked to sign the following agreement:

I wish to join JaguarMoon Cybercoven. As a Dedicant I will:

1. Work hard to learn the Craft for as long as I am associated with the coven;
2. Participate in at least 75% of the classes, rituals, and other required coven activities;
3. Meet on a regular basis with my Mentor to discuss my learning and growth within the coven;
4. Cultivate relationships of cooperation, friendship, and respect with other coven members;
5. Follow the Wiccan Rede: "An ye harm none, do as ye will";
6. Honor the Goddess and the God;
7. Work to protect and heal the Earth and Her creatures;
8. Use magick affecting other individuals only with their express consent;
9. Support my sisters and brothers within the coven in their learning, growth and aspirations;
10. Keep the identity of other coven members and friends confidential, except with their permission; and
11. Support the work of the coven with energy, money, or other resources, while giving first priority to the needs of my family and livelihood.

TAKING A PHYSICAL GROUP ONLINE

The Internet can be a valuable resource for your physical group, adding to the sharing and communication that is so vital to a group's sense of cohesion. Whether it's e-mail lists to facilitate information sharing, or Web pages to assist in the process of seeking new members (and screening them), cyber tools can make many aspects simpler for your group's membership.

The following is primarily for those of you who desire to transform some or all of your physical group's activities into the virtual realm. It is quite brief, and you may want to do your own research online, or look up *The Virtual Pagan*[1] for a deeper look at what is available and how to acquire it.

At least one member has to be passionate about the change. This person will be the key figure in helping the others understand the benefits of going online, and how to make good use of the potential of the Internet. Frankly, until most people understand this it will seem to be mumbo-jumbo and far too technical to bother with.

Start by discussing what you want from the Internet. How is it going to help you do what you want to do? Is it best as a signboard for seekers? A place to share information you feel is too important to keep within a small group? Do you want to start a Pagan news service, offer classes, or seek out past members? Your decisions will guide you to what you need.

If you wish to share information in a dynamic fashion, you may want to consider an e-mail list, or adding a message board to your Website. Some Web hosts offer e-mail addresses and the ability to host your own e-mail list as part of the hosting package.

If you simply wish to publish information, and perhaps request feedback, then a page on a Website will suffice.

If you want to attract seekers, then a Website is a good idea. You can place information about the tradition, goals, and structure, and what you are looking for in a seeker on one of more pages, and then have a Web-based application form on another.

If you would like the ability to hold "real-time" meetings without being face to face, IRC is a great program to use.

The existence of a magickal group on the Internet does not necessarily mean that it also inhabits the Web. Owning a domain is an advanced application. If you are either new to magickal group leadership or to Web-developing skills I advise that you wait at least until your group is in its second year before taking on these tasks. Or you may delegate them to another.

ShadowMoon did not create a Web presence until we entered our third year together. There were many factors in our decision, both good and bad, but in the end we decided that the benefits outweighed the risks. Some of the issues we discussed were:

- Privacy and confidentiality—not only of magickal group members' mundane information, but also of our teachings.

~Appendix E~

◉ Going "public" with our tradition and having to turn away potential students because of our teaching cycle.

◉ Financial issues of registration and rental of Web hosting services.

◉ Website creation and maintenance. Who would create the site, and and who will update and maintain it?

◉ How will disagreements as to how the information is presented be handled?

JaguarMoon, on the other hand, sees its Website as fulfilling several functions. It is a place where people can find out more about what a cyber coven is (and is not), it is a repository for a great deal of information we have found to be valuable, and it is a place where people can learn more about the class we teach. There was never any doubt that we would have a Website immediately upon forming the coven, partially because we had several members who were comfortable with computer technology and partially because it was important to us that the Website be a fully functional part of our cyber existence.

If you are not sure that you want to create a Web page right now, you may nevertheless purchase the domain name. This way you can protect a valuable asset (a domain name with great meaning to you), but you do not have to create a Web page or use the name in any public manner. Getting a domain name is probably sensible for a magickal group just beginning, or even one in its first year. I, for example, owned the domain name *jaguarmoon.org* for several months before placing a Website there because I decided to wait until after I had hived off the coven and it was fully birthed.

No one "owns" a domain name any more than someone "owns" a telephone number. You buy it for a set period of time and then renew your ownership annually. When you register the domain, you are asked for administrative, technical, and billing contacts. These are individuals who you trust to handle issues involving the domain name record. In many cases, the technical contact is a representative of your ISP (Internet Service Provider, which can include DSL service or cable) or Website host the administrative contact is a magickal group representative.

Your domain will be "hosted" by a provider. This means that you will have to rent a portion of storage on a very powerful computer (called a server), which then provides you with a piece of cyberspace on which to place your Website. Some Web service providers will register your domain name for you, at no extra charge. Drak.Net (*www.draknet.net*) is a wonderful, Pagan-friendly, Web-hosting site that also happens to provide excellent customer service at amazingly affordable prices.

If you do not wish to own a domain, or if your magickal group is just getting started, one solution is to have a group member maintain a Website for group use. This can turn into a problem if there is a disagreement as to how the information on the site is presented, or how often it is updated. No more than three people should be involved in the design of the site to avoid the "too many cooks" syndrome, and they should regularly check in with the magickal group's leaders as to how the site looks and feels. Remember that your Website will be an advertisement for your group, even if you do not design it for that purpose.

Nowadays you do not need to know HTML (hyper text markup language) to create a Web page. There are several programs that make it possible for you to design a beautiful Web page without ever looking at code. These programs have some flaws (such as not being able to incorporate .cgi scripts) but they are nonetheless very good at getting a Website created.

~Appendix E~

If you are going to create a Website, you will need to own an FTP (fixed transfer protocol) program. One I can recommend is WS-FTP, which you can download from *www.ipswitch.com*. This program will move files from your hard drive directory onto your Website with just a click of a button. It has great sounds, too!

As with anything computer-related, I recommend that you use your library as a resource. Even if its books are a few years old, the data does not change quite that quickly. A few pointers to keep in mind:

- Not everyone has a fast connection to the Internet. Designing your pages with few graphics makes them reader-friendly.

- Do not use "flash" or auto-loading sounds.

- Keep in mind that dark backgrounds and gothic fonts look lovely, but are darned hard to read. Be kind to your viewer, and make the font size at least 12pt and the color schemes harmonious.

- Make sure that the information you display is fair use, in the public domain, or used with permission.

- Make it easy to move from one page to another by using easy-to-find navigation buttons and links.

- Have an index so a visitor can jump right to a piece of information, rather than having to wander around your site.

- Take your time in building the site. It does not have to be the biggest and the best, at least not at first.

POSITIVE COMMUNICATION ONLINE

Because 99 percent of our online communication is through the written word, inherent problems arise because we have no auditory or psychic nuances. ("You are an idiot" said affectionately with a smile feels quite different from "you are an idiot" in black and white with no other cues.) Writing is a skill at which not all excel, leading the reader to interpret as vague or contradictory what seems crystal clear to the author. We bring our experiences to communication, so what seems commonplace to one writer can "push all the buttons" for an audience. Anything written only captures a moment in time—and we all have had moments we regret, later.

Some things to keep in mind about e-mail/text communication are:

E-mail is light speed, but people are not. If you don't get an immediate response, be patient (some of us can only read personal e-mail during the day, but we can't reply without going through hoops, for example). And, you don't have to immediately reply, even though the message is right there, *looking* at you.

~Magickal Connections~

Respect other people's level of communication. My mom has difficulty with e-mail—both because she has an advanced case of RSI (repetitive stress injury), so she does most of her computer work via verbal commands, and also because she is very unsure about technology. Any little thing that goes wrong turns into a major event for her. I know this, and I factor it in to my dealing with her.

Watch replies that capture the entire message when you're only focusing on one aspect, or sentence. Snip unnecessary text to save other's time and avoid clogging her/his inbox.

Pay attention to and use emoticons to better express your message. Emoticons are the "smiley faces" that you look at sideways or the grin <g> indicators people have developed to make text messages more expressive.

Pay attention to how you are emphasizing messages. ALL UPPERCASE IS CONSIDERED SHOUTING, and incredibly annoying to read for an entire message. (My masseuse uses uppercase, but she has a hard time reading most fonts, even with the viewer at maximum, so I forgive her.) Other ways to emphasize are to use on either side of a word ***this way*** and sometimes you'll see **%this%** or **>this<**.

Warn folks if you're going to post a very long e-mail (put "Long" in the subject line) or if you're going to rant (usually /rant on and /rant off).

Please don't forward jokes, pleas for money, virus warnings, and so forth. Maybe you'll want to make exceptions for Pagan-related jokes, but that is pretty much it. (Another hot button is chain letters—the messages that end with something such as "forward this to 10 people and you'll have blessings and abundance forever!" Grrrrr. I don't like to be coerced into doing anything, and those letters are rude.) If you are convinced a plea or warning is valuable, FIRST check to see if it's real. Go to Google (*www.google.com*) and type in some information—the name of the virus being warned about, for example, or key phrases from the warning. If it is legitimate, a respectable company (such as Symantec or the American Heart Association) will have information on its page. If it isn't legitimate, one of the various watchdog sites on the Net, such as Snopes.com (*www.snopes.com*), will likely have it noted.

Perception is everything. If you take little care for your word choice or content then you will be perceived badly. I'm not saying that you should run out and take a course in grammar, but I am asking you to pay attention to how your words might be seen by someone else. I'm also asking you not to get upset if someone misunderstands you. Spellchecking is nice, opening with a greeting is nice, ending with courtesy is nice... so, be nice.

A BASIC CURRICULUM OF WICCAN STUDIES

This Curriculum of Wiccan Studies encompasses nine areas of study. To earn a "degree" in Wicca, students would complete a minimum of 10 essays (six in required areas and four in electives chosen from any area or from ideas submitted by the student). Essays will combine scholarly study, personal opinion, and experience, with the length varying by topic. Sources, bibliographies, and/or reading lists will be cited, as appropriate, and may include books, magazines, Web documents, FAQs, and e-mail correspondence. Fellow students will review each essay, with comments, constructive critiques, and suggestions for further study provided. The completion of the six required areas of study grants a provisional degree, and the completion of the electives completes the course in Wiccan Studies.

~Magickal Connections~

Required Areas of Study

I. Essentials of Wicca

Write a 10-page essay on the Essentials of Wicca. The essay should primarily discuss personal beliefs and spirituality, including: basic spirituality and beliefs; a brief history of modern Wicca; magick and spellcraft; the Sabbats; the Rede and the three-fold law; the God and Goddess; and tools of the Craft.

II. Deity Studies

Write a five-page essay on one topic from the following list or on a topic of your choosing that relates to Deity: the Goddess and God; Pagan pantheons [select one from a particular culture (Norse, Egyptian, etc.)]; Goddess images and ideals in particular cultures; God images and ideals in particular cultures; fertility myths and Deities.

III. History

Write a five-page essay on one topic from the following list or on a topic of your choosing that relates to Wicca and witchcraft in history: origins of modern Wicca, ancient traditions and Earth-based/Pagan religions, witchcraft around the world, persecution through the ages.

IV. Rituals, Magick, and Spellcraft

Write a five-page essay on one topic from the following list or on a topic of your choosing that relates to rituals and magick: ritual design and construction (a how-to guide); magick, uses and abuses; personal experiences, successes and failures of spells; magick in literature; full moon rituals; rituals and spells in particular cultures; crystal magick; candle magick.

~Appendix G~

V. Ethics

Write a five-page essay on one topic from the following list or on a topic of your choosing that relates to Wiccan ethics: the Rede in theory and practice; creative writing—versions of the Rede; the ethical nature of Wicca.

VI. The Sabbats

Write a five-page essay on one topic from the following list or on a topic of your choosing that relates to the Sabbats: meanings of the Sabbats; Halloween; Sabbat ritual design.

Elective Courses of Study

VII. Comparative Studies

Write one or more (maximum of three) two- to five-page essays on topics from the following list or on topics of your choosing that relate to Comparative Studies: Pagan elements in Christianity; mythologies and legends across cultures; God and Goddess legends; comparison of Traditions (Celtic, Dianic, etc.); comparison of Pantheons (Egyptian vs. Celtic, Norse vs. Hindu, etc.); Wicca vs. Magick.

VIII. Fine Arts

Submit a Pagan-/Wiccan-themed portfolio of images or literature you have produced. Media may include drawings, paintings, crafts, poetry, and prose. A minimum of five examples should be submitted.

IX. Divination

Write one or more (maximum of three) two- to five-page essays on topics from the following list or on topics of your choosing that relate to divination: tarot; runes; scrying; astrology.

ADVANCED STUDENT LESSON PLAN FOR JAGUARMOON

This plan would be for all members of the coven who are at least First Degree Initiates and have a demonstrated understanding and mastery of the subjects outlined in the first year curriculum. The focus here is on Wicca—not much of other religions/traditions—and would not necessarily be limited to a single year. Each course of study could be done individually or as a group process.

Magick—Uses and Abuses

A combination of ethical exploration and spell design: bindings and banishings, when to step in and when to walk away.

Personal Experiences—Successes and Failures of Spells

We frequently do magick, but are not so disciplined at tracking results. This module is a quarterly dialogue about both personal and group ritual results.

~Magickal Connections~

Magick in Literature

How is magick perceived and used? This is a multi-genre topic and likely takes place within a discussion group. It includes looking at Pagan publications and what is presented there. Who uses magick? How do they use it? Is there a bias?

Rituals and Spells in Particular Cultures

Research is the focus of this module. Why and/or how are cultural spells different? The same? Mythology of cultures is would be appropriate for in-depth research in this module.

Deity Perception

How do we experience the God/dess in our lives? As we grow older how do our perceptions change? Whom have we identified with over the years? Do the God/desses have qualities we should emulate? Avoid? Moving beyond Duality into the One.

Reincarnation and Past Lives

Evidence for/proof of? Doing meditations, reviewing memories, etc. Karmic ties and agreements. Evaluating where you are in the time/space continuum.

Meaning of the Sabbats

There is a wealth of meaning embodied in these Wiccan holy days. This as an advanced class in which we learn the Mysteries associated with/explained by the ritual of each of the eight Sabbats are discussed in detail.

~Appendix H~

Living Wiccan

How do we live our faith? Problems encountered; battles fought in public and private; support for Pagans partnered with non-Pagan spousal units. This is another ongoing assignment in which we meet monthly to discuss changes we've made or are making to bring our lives more into alignment with the Wiccan Rede. It is also be a further exploration of our roles as Priest/esses with and within our larger communities. As well, ongoing discussions and modules in: tarot, runes scrying, astrology, Qabala, crystal magick, healing, and herbs.

NOTES

Introduction

1. See the Bibliography for full references.
2. GreyCat, *Deepening Witchcraft*, "A Community of Like-Minded People: Building Community," Chapter 12.

Chapter I

1. A cyber magickal group is one that holds most, if not all, of its practices online. This may include studies, teaching, rituals, and/or information sharing.
2. Forsyth, *Group Dynamics, 2nd edition*.
3. I have since come to understand the non-fluffy aspect of the Fae, those elemental beings of a very different nature than Disney's version.
4. I use this phrase to include both aspects of the Divine.
5. The phrase *power-over* comes from Starhawk and her brilliant examination of magickal group dynamics in *Truth or Dare*.

6. From their Website (*www.reclaiming.org/about/index.html*), under "About Reclaiming." Used with permission.
7. Ibid.

Chapter 2

1. For example, Starhawk's *The Spiral Dance*, Amber K's *CovenCraft*, or Edain McCoy's *Inside a Witches' Coven*. See the Bibliography for full references.

Chapter 3

1. "Julia" from the PaganPath list. 1999.
2. Del Ray, 1987.
3. I highly recommend Eugene Kennedy's *On Becoming A Counselor: A Basic Guide for Nonprofessional Counselors and Other Helpers*.
4. I again strongly recommend Kennedy's *On Becoming a Counselor*. There are also some wonderful seminars and classes, often listed under "Management," at your local college or university's extension program.
5. To my knowledge, cyber groups whose only purpose is to perform ritual and that otherwise have limited communication between members have not been very successful. Online, the energy is not as strong and tangible as that formed by physical contact. I believe that, unless the energy of a cyber group is maintained through daily conversation and interaction, it will fail. A physical magickal group can meet only monthly and succeed, but a cyber magickal group simply will not.

6. This exercise was created by my good friend Diana Rajchel.

Chapter 4

1. Bass, *Stogdill's Handbook of Leadership*.
2. Lewin, Lippit, and White. "Patterns of aggressive behavior in experimentally created social climates."

Chapter 5

1. I highly recommend Anodea Judith and Selene Vega's *The Sevenfold Journey*.
2. Fortune, *Applied Magic*, p. 37.
3. Ibid.

Chapter 6

1. I am indebted to Judy Harrow's *Spiritual Mentoring* for assisting me in clarifying my thoughts on this topic. I also strongly recommend it for anyone engaged in a mentoring relationship.

2. Harrow, *Spiritual Mentoring*, p. 51.

3. Samaritans of New York City, *http://www.samaritansnyc.org*

4. Baldwin, *Calling the Circle*.

Chapter 7

1. Peck, *The Different Drum: Community Making and Peace*, p. 59.
2. These three exercises come from a friend of a friend (who wishes to remain anonymous), who

uses them when team-building for the climbing expeditions he leads.

Chapter 8

1. Sexuality in ritual is, in and of itself, not an automatically bad thing. In this case, however, sex was this predator's vehicle for domination and manipulation, not worship.
2. Bees are sacred to Demeter.
3. I developed this exercise after reading a similar one in Diane Mariechild's wonderful book, *InnerDance*.

Chapter 9

1. Quoted in Adams, "Shoot to Not Kill."
2. PaganLibrary.com. This is a reference from "HPS Disease," a humorous poem by Vivienne West that begins:

   "I am the leader of this group / And before Me all you others stoop / Bend thou, adore Me on your knees / For I have HPS disease!"
3. Exercises based on the work of Leonard Felder and Scott Peck, M.D.

Chapter 10

1. Anonymous. Copied into my journal at the age of 16.
2. See the Bibliography for full references.
3. See the Bibliography for full references.

Appendix E

1. Mc Sherry, *The Virtual Pagan*, Chapter Two.

BIBLIOGRAPHY

Adams, Eric Adams. "Shoot to Not Kill." *Popular Science Magazine*, May 2003. *www.popsci.com/popsci/science/64c7359b9fa84010vgnvcm1000004eecbccdrcrd.html*, accessed July 2006.

Baldwin, Christine. *Calling the Circle.* New York: Bantam New Age, 1998.

Bass, Bernard. *Stogdill's Handbook of Leadership: A Survey of Theory and Research.* New York: Free Press, 1989.

Cunningham, Scott. *Earth Power.* St. Paul, Minn.: Llewellyn Publications, 1985.

———. *Wicca: A Guide For The Solitary Practitioner.* St. Paul, Minn.: Llewellyn Publications, 1994.

Farrar, Janet, and Stewart Farrar. *The Witches' Bible.* Blaine, Wash.: Phoenix Publications, 1984.

———. *What Witches Do.* Blaine, Wash.: Phoenix Publications, 1991.

~Magickal Connections~

Felder, Leonard. *Does Someone At Work Treat You Badly?* New York: Berkley, 1993.

Forsyth, D. R. *Group Dynamics (2nd edition).* Pacific Grove, Calif.: Brooks/Cole, 1990.

Fortune, Dion. *Applied Magic.* York Beach, Maine: Weiser Books, 2000.

GreyCat. *Deepening Witchcraft: Advancing Skills and Knowledge.* Toronto: ECW Press, 2002.

Harrow, Judy. *Spiritual Mentoring: A Pagan Guide.* Toronto: ECW Press, 2002.

Haugk, Kenneth C. *Antagonists in the Church: How to Identify and Deal with Destructive Conflict.* Minneapolis: Ausburg Publishing House, 1988.

Judith, Anodea, and Selene Vega. *The Sevenfold Journey.* Berkeley, Calif.: The Crossing Press, 1993.

K, Amber. *Covencraft.* St. Paul, Minn.: Llewellyn Publications, 1998.

Kennedy, Eugene. *On Becoming A Counselor: A Basic Guide for Nonprofessional Counselors and Other Helpers (Third Edition).* New York: Crossroad Publishing, 2001.

Lewin, K., R. Lippit, and R. K. White. "Patterns Of Aggressive Behavior In Experimentally Created Social Climates." *Journal of Social Psychology, 10, 271–301.*

Mariechild, Diane. *InnerDance.* Berkeley, Calif.: The Crossing Press, 1987.

———. *MotherWit.* Berkeley, Calif.: The Crossing Press, 1981.

McCoy, Edain. *Inside a Witches' Coven.* St. Paul, Minn.: Llewellyn Publications, 1997.

Mc Sherry, Lisa. *CyberCoven.Org: Creating and Maintaining a Magickal Group Online, Second Edition. www.cybercoven.org.* 2004.

~Bibliography~

————. *The Virtual Pagan: Exploring Wicca and Paganism Through the Internet.* York Beach, Maine: Red Wheel/ Weiser, 2002.

O'Gaea, Ashleen. *Raising Witches: Teaching the Wiccan Faith to Children.* Franklin Lakes, N.J.: New Page Books, 2006.

PaganLibrary.com. www.paganlibrary.com/humor/ hps_disease.php, accessed July 2006.

Peck, Scott M. *The Different Drum: Community Making and Peace.* New York: Simon and Schuster, 1998.

————. *The Road Less Traveled: A New Psychology of Love, Traditional Values and Spiritual Growth.* New York: Simon and Schuster, 1978.

RavenWolf, Silver. *To Ride A Silver Broomstick.* St. Paul, Minn.: Llewellyn Publications, 1994.

Starhawk. *The Spiral Dance: A Rebirth of the Ancient Religion of the Great Goddess.* San Francisco: Harper San Francisco, 1979.

————. *Truth or Dare: Encounters with Power, Authority, and Mystery.* San Francisco: Harper San Francisco, 1987.

INDEX

A

accepting a protégé, 103-104
active listening, 125-126
administration, group, 54-55
advertise, places to, 37-38
advertisement,
  creating an, 36
advertising, 36
advertising online, 39
after the first year, 183-186
Anarchist and Discordian
  groups, 27
anger within the circle,
  159-164
anger, exercises
  for dealing with, 163-164

antagonists,
  defusing, 151
  natural, 149-151
Applied Magic, 88
artistic expression, 188
asking the God/dess, 62-64
assessment,
  leadership style, 76-77
astral temple, 90-92
  ritual, creating an, 92-93
  describing our, 91-93
attention esteem
  exercise, 112
authoritarian, 71-73

~Index~

ABOUT THE AUTHOR

Lisa Mc Sherry has worked with groups of many sizes and structures since her introduction to witchcraft in 1981. The leader of her own group since 2000, she has used her role to test her theories and develop them for wider contexts. A sextuple Virgo, she uses her organizational skills in writing about the occult and its dynamics in a practical, accessible fashion. She is a popular speaker at conferences throughout the United States and Canada, and her writings can be found online through *www.cybercoven.org*. Mc Sherry resides near Seattle, Washington. She can be reached at *lisa@cybercoven.org*.